SAVED BY GRACE

THE ESSENCE OF CHRISTIANITY

JACK
COTTRELL

CONTENTS

INTRODUCTION

From the beginning of my teaching career at Cincinnati Bible Seminary (fall 1967), I taught a graduate course on the doctrine of grace. For the first couple of years it was called "New Testament Theology," since Dean Lewis Foster wanted me to teach a course on that subject. I asked him how he wanted me to develop the subject, and he said, "Any way you like." (Thank you!) So I decided to teach the grace concepts that had been forming in my mind over the previous five years or so, and I presented this material following the progression of Paul's thought in Romans 1 through 8. I soon changed the name of the course to simply "The Doctrine of Grace."

Over my 49 years of teaching at Cincinnati Bible Seminary (now Cincinnati Christian University), I taught "The Doctrine of Grace" at least 80 times, to close to 2,000 students, all the while refining and expanding the content.

My first book on grace was published in 1976. At that time Standard Publishing (SP) was producing a small book of Bible study lessons each quarter as an alternative to the regular lesson quarterlies used by multitudes of churches. These small books followed the International Sunday School Lesson Scripture texts used by the regular quarterlies. (These texts were and still are selected by a standing committee of the National Council of Churches.) I was happy to receive an invitation from SP to write one of these books for an upcoming quarter.

The unfortunate thing about this is that I had no choice as to the selection or order of the texts to be covered. The good thing, though, was that the theme around which the texts were chosen was salvation by grace! So I gladly accepted the offer to write the book. Each chapter was an essay on the general emphasis of that week's text, and not a verse-by-verse explanation of the text. That way I was able to cover most of the general grace topics, though not in a systematic order.

That little book (96pp., pb., $1.95!) was given the title, *Being Good Enough Isn't Good Enough.* I did not come up with that title, but I thought it sounded pretty "catchy." (Later I realized that the statement is actually not true. If a person *could* be "good enough," that would by definition BE "good enough." The problem is that no one CAN be good enough to be saved.) When SP's supply ran out, College Press (CP) agreed to publish the book as *13 Lessons on Grace* (1988, 103pp., pb.). It is still available under that title through Wipf and Stock Publishers (Eugene, OR, 2001).

Over the years my developing thoughts on grace appeared in parts of other books, especially these: *What the Bible Says About God the Redeemer* (CP, 1987), *Baptism: A Biblical Study* (CP, 1989), *The College Press NIV Commentary, Romans* (2 vols., 1996, 1998), and *The Faith Once for All* (CP, 2002). Then I decided to publish a comprehensive theological study of grace, following the outline and content I was using for my seminary course. The result was *Set Free! What the Bible Says About Grace*, published by CP in 2009 (401pp. hb.). This is my definitive work on the subject.

All the while I was teaching and writing about grace on a more-or-less academic level, I was everywhere teaching about it in local churches and regional seminars. In that kind of venue I developed a series of lessons that I have used dozens of time (and still use), just to help people in the churches understand the nature of their salvation. This little book now in your hands contains the gist of these lessons, along with some other material. I will now explain what is included here.

Part One of this book is a series of ten lessons I call "Grace Distinctions." This description comes from my 60 years of studying and teaching theology, during which I have come to think of theology as "the art of making distinctions." I have especially found that a proper understanding of grace requires making some very important distinctions. When I was teaching grace in the seminary, I came to the point where my beginning lectures for the course were an exposition of these distinctions. The ten lessons in the first section of this book are intended to set forth this material. Sometimes the same ideas will come up again in Part Two.

The main section of this book is Part Two ("Grace Accomplished and Applied"), which is a series of 14 lessons on what it means to be "saved by grace." These lessons are presented in a simple and orderly manner that I hope can be understood by anyone: prospective

Christians, new Christians, seasoned Christians. These lessons can be used for evangelistic purposes, for small group studies, for personal devotions, or for sermon ideas. (I do recommend that teachers, preachers, and group leaders using this for such purposes *also* use and study the larger volume mentioned above, *Set Free!*, using the table of contents and the indexes to find more extensive developments of the subjects given in more abbreviated form in this small book.)

My goal and prayer is this: May God use this little book (through you, the reader) to reach multitudes with the message of His grace, and to lead them to a richer and deeper understanding of the "blessed assurance" of salvation.

JACK COTTRELL – SEPTEMBER 2017

PART ONE

GRACE
DISTINCTIONS

1. GOD AS CREATOR AND GOD AS SAVIOR

The first distinction relevant to the doctrine of grace is *how we relate to God*. In fact, just about everything begins with how you think of God. See this quote from James Orr: "The doctrine of God, it need scarcely be said, lies at the foundation of all right thinking in religion. In strictness, theology is just the doctrine of God. That is the meaning of the word. God is the Alpha and Omega of theological study, for as a man thinks about his God so will his theology be all through. It is not too strong to say that, in principle, every question of importance which arises in theology is already practically settled in the doctrine of God and His attributes. So essential is it to begin with Scripturally right thoughts about God." (*Sidelights on Christian Doctrine*, London: Marshall Brothers, 1909; p. 8.)

People often occupy more than one role in life; as we sometimes say, they wear two or more hats. Thus you may relate to the same person in two different ways. E.g., someone you know may be a police officer during the week, and your Bible school teacher on Sunday. Just so, God wears at least two MAIN hats, representing two of his main kinds of works and two of his main relationships with us.

First of all and primarily, God is our **CREATOR**, and we are his *creatures*. In this role he may be thought of as wearing a construction worker's "hard hat." But then, as Creator, he also has other roles or other "hats." Isaiah 33:22 names some of the things God does in his ongoing role as Creator: "Yahweh is our Judge; Yahweh is our Lawgiver; Yahweh is our King." James 4:12 says it thus: "There is only one Lawgiver and Judge—the One who is able to save and to destroy."

Because he is our Creator, God has absolute ownership and absolute authority over us; he is our Ruler, our Lord, and our King. He has the right to tell us what to do and to enforce his orders. In this way he is our Lawgiver, as Isaiah and James say. In this role he gives us instructions and commandments that we are absolutely obligated to obey. These commandments cover the areas of ethics and worship. Also, the fact that God is our Judge motivates us to obey the law commands which he gives us as Creator.

All of this is true, and it all applies totally apart from any thought of sin and salvation. Before sin entered, God's relation to Adam and Eve was Creator-to-creature. And even after sin has come into the picture, much of our own relation to God is Creator-to-creature. This includes our obligation to submit to his lordship and to obey his commands.

But the fact that sin is now present means that God has taken on another role in his relationship with the human race: because we are *sinners*, he is now our **SAVIOR**. This role is necessary because sin has entered into and permeated the creation. Here we see God fulfilling two separate sub-roles in order to bring about our salvation, because sin causes the sinner two kinds of problems. We call this the "double curse" of sin. And since different problems require different answers, God our Savior responds to both with his "double cure."

First of all, because sin is transgression of God's law, it makes us guilty and brings us under the law's penalty, which is eternal condemnation to hell. These are *legal* problems. To save us from this fate, God takes on the role of *Redeemer.* This word is not just a synonym for *Savior.* Redemption is a specific kind of salvation. "To redeem" means to set something or someone free from captivity by paying a price. God does this specifically in his incarnation as Jesus the Christ. Through his substitutionary atonement, Jesus paid the penalty for the sins of the world. This redemptive accomplishment is then applied to sinners in the form of *justification* (or forgiveness). Justification is an act of the Judge, in which he tells the sinner, "No penalty for you," and thus cancels his eternal condemnation. (When I think of God in his role as Redeemer, I think of him as wearing a fire-fighter's hat – because he [God the Son incarnate as Jesus] extinguishes the fires of hell for us.)

In addition to this, God our SAVIOR has a second sub-role, in which he responds to the second part of the double curse that has affected us sinners. This second sin-problem is the fact that our very natures, especially our souls, have become corrupted and infected with the disease of sin (see Jeremiah 17:9). Thus God must now take on this other saving role: the role of *Healer.* (Here I think of him as wearing the garb of a physician or surgeon.) This saving work of healing is accomplished mainly by the person of the Holy Spirit, who in this New Covenant era has come to dwell within us for this very purpose. In the very moment when the Spirit enters into us (in baptism, Acts 2:38), he *regenerates* us: i.e., he raises us from spiritual death into new life. From that moment on he indwells us in order to *sanctify* us, helping us to overcome the stubborn remains of the sin-disease.

The key point is this: in some aspects or circumstances of our lives, we are relating to God primarily as *creature to Creator.* As our Creator, God is our King, Lawgiver, and Judge. But in other parts of our lives, we are relating to God primarily as *sinner to Savior.* As our Savior, God is our Redeemer and Healer.

As Creator and as Savior, God is always BOTH to us. It is not the case that *sometimes* he is our Creator, and *sometimes* he is our Savior. He is always our Creator, and always our Savior. Yet it is very important to discern which *aspects* of our lives relate to God in the former role (e.g., obeying his law commandments), and which relate to him in the latter role (e.g., praying a prayer of repentance).

2. LAW CODES VS. THE LAW SYSTEM

In this second grace distinction, we are speaking about Paul's use of the Greek word for "law," namely, NOMOS. He uses this term many times, especially in Romans and Galatians. See, e.g., Romans 2:12-15; 3:19-20; 3:27-28; 6:14-15; 8:1-4; Galatians 2:16. Here I am emphasizing a crucial distinction, namely, the distinction between LAW CODES and the LAW SYSTEM.

Understanding this distinction is essential for a proper understanding of grace. Unfortunately, you will almost never see anyone talking about it. It is virtually unrecognized. But I stress (holler! yell!) this at you: in Paul's use of "nomos" (law) you MUST distinguish between law codes and the law system.

When Paul refers to "law," most of the time he means law codes (the Law of Moses, for example). A law code is simply the complete list or set of commands given to us by God in his role as CREATOR, which includes his rights and role as Lawgiver. We as his creatures are under absolute obligation to obey whatever law code he applies to us.

Which law code one is under depends on the historical circumstances under which one lives. In general, all age-of-accountability human beings are under the law code written on all hearts by virtue of our being created in God's image (Romans 2:14-15). In addition to that, all Israelites existing between Moses and Christ were under the Law of Moses as their unique law code. In this New Covenant age, we have a different collection of commands and instructions on how to live holy lives; this is our New Covenant law code. It consists of the instructions on holy living as found mainly in the New Testament.

This means that, yes, we as Christians are under a law code, consisting of commands that we are absolutely obligated to obey. There are no exceptions, since we are creatures of the Creator and Lawgiver. We are always related to God as our Creator.

Sometimes, though, when Paul uses the word "nomos" (law), he is not referring to any law code as such, but to what I call the LAW SYSTEM. The law system (and there is only one) is the method or program by which one may be right with God, i.e., the method or program why which one may actually enter heaven—by how well he obeys his law code. In other words, totally apart from any consideration of grace or of Jesus Christ, one may be right with God solely in terms of his law code. How this works is what I am calling the law system. (See the next chapter below.)

An analogy for these two uses of the word "law" is the way we use the word "medicine." Sometimes this word means the pills and capsules and tonics we take in doses. Here we speak in the plural; these are our various "medicines." But sometimes the word "medicine" (singular) is used to mean the WAY or METHOD of treating illnesses (as contrasted with, e.g., prayer, sorcery, or positive thinking). This latter use would refer to the "field of medicine."

Likewise, a law code is composed of specific laws or commands, whereas the law system is a WAY of being right with God, a way of getting into heaven. It is crucial to know which of these uses Paul has in mind when he uses "nomos" (which is usually translated "law").

3. THE LAW SYSTEM VS. THE GRACE SYSTEM

In the previous chapter we spoke of the "law system" as a way of being right with God and as a way of getting into heaven, as something distinct from a "law code." But this is not the only such "system" (for which we will be eternally thankful!). There is also the "grace system," which is another, entirely different way of being right with God. It is important to understand that these "systems" are indeed two ways of receiving eternal life and going to heaven. From our perspective as sinners, we can think of this simply as salvation. Thus the point here is this: we must distinguish between two ways or systems of being "saved," i.e., of getting to heaven. These two ways are the LAW SYSTEM (as mentioned in chapter two above) and the GRACE SYSTEM.

This may well be the most important distinction of the ten I am explaining here. It is the key to Paul's point in Romans 6:14-15, where he says twice that we are "not under law but under grace." NOT UNDER LAW! BUT UNDER GRACE! This is indeed one of the most important things you can know about yourself: you are not under law, but under grace! What does this mean?

This means that we as Christians are not under the LAW SYSTEM of salvation; we are under the GRACE SYSTEM of salvation. We are not trying to be right with God by how well we are keeping our law code (i.e., by "how good" we are), but we are right with God via the gift of grace made possible through Jesus Christ. If you do not get this distinction between the law system and the grace system, you will never understand grace.

Many still think wrongly that in this statement ("you are not under law"), Paul is talking about a law CODE. Some think he means we are not under the Law of Moses. It is true that we are not under the Law of Moses as our law code, but that is NOT what he is talking about here. Some think Paul means that we as Christians are not obligated to obey ANY law code, now that we are under grace. This is absolutely not the idea. God is still our Creator; we still have a law code; we are under that law code as a way of living.

Here is what Paul is saying: we are not under the law SYSTEM, where our *salvation* would depend on how well we keep our law code. The problem with trying to be "saved" (trying to be right with our Creator) via the law system is that for this to happen you would have to obey your law code perfectly! You would have to be 100% good! This of course will never happen for us, since all are already sinners (Romans 3:23). The sad fact is that no one CAN be right with God under the law system.

Remember: we relate to God as Creator and Lawgiver in many ways, and we relate to his law in many positive ways. But for *salvation* purposes, we are not relating to God as Creator and Lawgiver, and we are not under law in this sense. We are relating to him as Savior and Redeemer, depending only on his grace. "We are not under law but under grace" means that we are not under the law *system*; we are under the grace *system*! Here is the summary of this distinction:

A. Under the law system, God as Creator, acting through his holiness, gives us our law code. Perfect obedience to our law code results in heaven; disobedience to it (even once) results in hell.

B. Under the grace system, God as Savior, acting through his love, gives us Jesus. Faith in Jesus results in heaven; unbelief toward Jesus results in hell.

The following chart shows this same contrast between the two systems of being right with God:

THE LAW SYSTEM VS. THE GRACE SYSTEM

I. THE LAW SYSTEM	II. THE GRACE SYSTEM
A. God as CREATOR, acting through HIS *HOLINESS*, gives us our <u>LAW CODE</u> –	A. God as SAVIOR, acting through HIS *LOVE*, gives us <u>JESUS</u> –
B. Perfect obedience to which results in <u>HEAVEN</u>!	B. Faith in whom results in <u>HEAVEN</u>!
Disobedience to which (even one sin) results in <u>HELL</u>!	Unbelief toward whom results in <u>HELL</u>!

---

4. LAW COMMANDS VS. GRACE COMMANDS

The fourth distinction is between two kinds of commands given by God: law commands, and grace commands. (The latter can also be called GOSPEL commands.) A command is a grammatical imperative, stated in the imperative mood (or mode, as distinct from indicative, interrogative, and exclamatory modes). It is a verbal communication in which someone is ordering or instructing another person to DO something.

Much of God's communication with us is in the form of commands, and much of our relationship with God consists of responding to these commands. This response can be either positive (obedience) or negative (disobedience).

The important thing to remember is this: God's commands or imperatives to us are not all of the same kind. He gives us TWO KINDS of commands, depending on which hat he is wearing: his Creator hat, or his Savior hat. This distinction is crucial!

Sometimes God as our Creator gives instructions to us as his creatures. These instructions are LAW commands; they constitute our LAW CODE. As creatures of the Creator, we are under absolute obligation to obey these commands. This obligation never goes away.

On the other hand, sometimes God in his role as Savior gives instructions to us as sinners. These instructions are GRACE commands (or GOSPEL commands). They are God's answer to the sinner's question (as in Acts 2:37 and Acts 16:30), "What must I do to be saved?" When God answers such a question with imperatives, these imperatives are not intended to express his lordship over us; they are meant to tell us what we must do to receive the gift of his saving grace.

That such gospel commands exist is the necessary implication of the references to OBEDIENCE to the GOSPEL in several Biblical texts. In Romans 10:16, Paul says many Jews are lost because "they have not all obeyed the gospel" (literal translation, from the ESV). In 2 Thessalonians 1:8 Paul says Jesus will come again "inflicting vengeance" on those "who do not obey the gospel of our Lord Jesus." In 1 Peter 4:17 the Apostle asks, "What will be the outcome for those who do not obey the gospel of God?"

Some wrongly assume that the "gospel of our Lord Jesus" contains only the facts of his death, burial, and resurrection (see 1 Corinthians 15:1-4). This, however, is an unbiblical limitation on the word "gospel." The gospel (good news) includes these gospel *facts*, but it also includes gospel *promises* (see Col. 1:5, 23) and gospel *commands*—as seen above. One does not obey facts or promises; one obeys commands. Part of the gospel is the commands that tell us how to be saved.

Law commands and gospel commands are very different. An analogy is the difference between imperatives from government representatives ("Stop in the name of the law!"), and imperatives from one's doctor ("Take this medicine! Also, lose 30 pounds!"). In both cases these instructions are commands, given in the imperative mode. In both cases, they "tell you what to do," but for very different reasons.

In summary, when the Creator-God gives instructions to us as his creatures, he is giving us law commands; when the Savior-God instructs us as sinners on how to be saved, he is giving us grace (i.e., gospel) commands.

5. OBEDIENCE TO LAW VS. OBEDIENCE TO GRACE

This next distinction grows directly out of the previous one. If there are two kinds of commands, then there must be TWO KINDS OF OBEDIENCE. Most of the time our obedience is the way we respond to the Creator's law commands. We are simply obeying our everyday law code. E.g., every time we speak the truth, we are obeying a law command of God (Ephesians 4:25). Honest payment of taxes is obedience to God's law (Romans 13:6-7). Living peaceably with our neighbors is obedience to our law code (Romans 12:18). Not doing things that are forbidden by the Creator is also obedience to law commands (e.g., not stealing, not using bad language—Ephesians 4:28-29). Our law code includes literally hundreds of such commands, and we are living in constant yet mostly unconscious obedience to them.

On the other hand, especially when we are in the process of becoming a Christian, we are obeying the GOSPEL commands. God gives us these commands not because he is the boss and not just because he wants to inform us of how a good human being is supposed to live. And we obey these gospel commands not simply to please our Creator, but because we want to be saved from our sins.

These grace commands show us the way to be saved; they tell us what WE must do to receive salvation.

This second kind of obedience is called "obeying the gospel." Twice Paul says that failure to obey the gospel is a main reason why people are not saved. As noted earlier, speaking specifically of Jews who were lost, he says, "They have not all obeyed the gospel" (Romans 10:16, literally translated). Speaking in general Paul says that at Christ's return he will inflict "vengeance on those who do not...obey the gospel" (2 Thessalonians 1:8). See again 1 Peter 4:17.

Obeying the gospel includes doing all the things the Savior-God says the sinner must do to receive salvation. This includes believing on Jesus (John 3:16; Acts 16:31); repenting of sin (Luke 13:3; Acts 2:38); confessing Jesus as Lord (Romans 10:9-10); and being immersed into Christ (Acts 2:38; Acts 22:16). Even as Christians we continue to obey the gospel commands to believe and repent, as we nurture in our hearts the ongoing attitudes of faith in Jesus and repentance toward sin.

Every act (and attitude) of obedience, including obedience to law commands AND obedience to grace commands, is a human work in the general sense of "something we do." Faith itself is a work in this sense, as is baptism. Yet such "works" (things we do) are perfectly consistent with grace since they are not obedience to law commands, but obedience to the grace commands of God as Savior. (See the next chapter.)

Obedience to gospel commands is like a rescuer saving a drowning man by throwing him a rope and yelling "Grab this rope!"

Technically that's a command, but grabbing the rope and being pulled to safety are pure grace. Another analogy is a group of fire-fighters on the ground holding a net under a third-story window in a burning building, and yelling "Jump!" to a woman trapped in the building. In this case "Jump!" is not a law command but a grace command, and the person obeys the command in order to be saved.

6. GENERAL WORKS VS. WORKS OF LAW

In our desire to understand grace, it is absolutely essential that we have a proper understanding of the term "works." This is because Ephesians 2:8-9 specifically says that because we are saved by grace through faith, we cannot be saved by works. So we must know what "works" means in this statement.

The problem is that most people have no idea what Paul means when he makes this statement. That is because they assume that whenever the Bible uses the term "works," it simply means "something you do," i.e., something YOU do in contrast with something GOD does. This assumption is seriously false.

In this case the distinction is not about the works that we do as such, but about the term "works" itself, and how the term is used. The fact is that when the New Testament uses terminology involving "works," it uses these terms in two distinct senses. This means that one of the most important (yet perhaps the least known) distinctions we must make in reference to grace is this: we must distinguish between the times when the New Testament uses "works" in a GENERAL or generic sense, and the times when it uses "works" in the more specific sense of WORKS OF LAW.

"Works" in the general or generic sense means simply "something you do." That includes ANYTHING you do, and THAT includes anything you do in obedience to any command of God, whether that is a law command of God as Creator or a grace command of God as Savior. I.e., faith itself is something YOU do, and thus it is a work in this sense. This is proved by John 6:26-29, where Jesus uses "works" terminology to describe faith itself. Faith, along with every other act of obedience to grace commands, is a work in this generic sense.

But here's the deal: Paul distinguishes faith from works (as in Ephesians 2:8-9 and many other places), and says that works have no place in receiving grace. How can this be so, in view of John 6:26-29? Simply thus: when Paul uses the term "works," he is not using it in the generic sense of "something you do." For him, it *must* have some other meaning—a more specific meaning. Otherwise his teaching would be in conflict with the teaching of Jesus—which cannot be. Thus we must distinguish how *Paul* is using the term "works," from how *Jesus* is using the term.

The crucial point is this: *whenever* Paul uses the term "works," he specifically means "works of law." Sometimes he says "works"; sometimes he says "works of law"—but he always means "works of law." (A careful study of Romans 3:27 – 4:8 shows this. In Romans 4:6 he speaks of "being counted righteous"—i.e., justified—"apart from works," without adding "of law"; but it is clear that he means the same thing by "works" in 4:6 as he means by "works of law" in 3:28.) And for Paul, "works" is a specific category of "things we do," in the sense that *some* things we do are NOT "works"—i.e., not *works of law.*

See Romans 3:20, 28; Galatians 2:16; and 3:2, 5 for Paul's use of the term "works of law." E.g., in Romans 3:20 he says that "by works of law no flesh will be justified in God's sight." In Romans 3:28 he says we are "justified by faith apart from works of law." In Galatians 2:16 Paul repeats the thoughts of Romans 3:20, 28, and uses "works of law" three times. In Galatians 3:2 he asks whether we have received the Spirit "by works of law or by hearing with faith" (see v. 5 also).

Note: despite faulty translations, Paul NEVER uses an article in this phrase. He never says "THE works of THE law"; it is always just "works of law." Also, he is NEVER limiting this "law" to the Law of Moses, contrary to a common but seriously false interpretation. Here is the crucial point: the "works of law" (i.e., the "works" which cannot save) are ANY and ALL things we do in response to our law code (law commands), including all New Testament commands on holy living. Paul even includes our SINS against our law code in the concept of "works of law," as a comparison of Romans 3:28 and 4:6-8 shows. I.e., we are justified by faith, APART FROM a consideration of the record of our obedience to and of our sins against the commands of our law code. (Please read that last sentence carefully.)

So what are the "things we do" that are *not* included in the term "works" as Paul uses that term? Simply put, he does not include *obedience to the gospel* in the category of works (i.e., works of law). This must be so since we are not saved by works (Ephesians 2:8-9), but we *cannot be saved without* obedience to the gospel (Romans 10:16; 2 Thessalonians 1:8).

Here is the bottom line: when Paul says we are not saved by works, he means we are not saved by how well we obey our LAW commands. (This is *why* he calls them works OF LAW.) He is NOT, however, excluding acts of obedience to GRACE commands from the salvation event, including the command to be baptized. Obedience to gospel commands are not works, in Paul's sense of the term.

A final comment: what we are saying here does not mean that every "thing we do" belongs to ONE of these categories but not the OTHER. It means that one of the categories (and the term that applies to it as Jesus uses it—the generic "works") includes ALL things that we do, while the other category (and its descriptive term as Paul uses it—specifically "works of law") includes MOST of these same things, but not all of them. Paul reserves the term "works" for things we do in obedience to law commands.

7. THE LAW'S COMMANDS VS. THE LAW'S PENALTIES

Another distinction related to law is the distinction between the COMMANDS of the law, and the PENALTIES prescribed by the law when its commands are not obeyed. It is crucial to understand this distinction, in order to properly understand the work of Jesus Christ.

Any set of laws (any law code) contains both commands and penalties. See again Isaiah 33:22 and James 4:12: God is both LAWGIVER (giving commands) and JUDGE (enforcing obedience via penalties). As the former, in his role as Creator, God sets forth the commands he requires his creatures to obey. As the latter, also in his role as Creator, God sits in judgment on his creatures and applies the penalty of hell to the disobedient.

As far as we creatures are concerned, we are considered RIGHTEOUS when we obey the commands of the law. (Righteousness by definition means conformity to the relevant norm, and the relevant norm for human beings is the Creator's law.) If we maintain perfect obedience to our law code, we remain in fellowship with the Creator. But if we sin, we are no longer "right with God" in terms of the law's COMMANDS.

Does the law then become dysfunctional and disgraced when we sin against it? Does it fall apart in dishonor and impotence? No! The law, i.e., the Lawgiver, is prepared to deal with lawbreakers. The application of the law's PENALTY maintains the Lawgiver's honor and the law's ability to function. And with the application of the law's penalty, even the lawbreaker remains "right with the law" in the sense that he satisfies its required penalty. (As an analogy, we say that a criminal who serves his assigned term in prison has "paid his debt to society." In the case of God's law, however, the payment of the debt—eternity in hell—never ends.)

What does this have to do with God? Why does God's law include both commands AND penalties? It is a matter of God's own RIGHTEOUSNESS. Since God is the origin of the law, our response to that law reflects on God himself. Thus for God to maintain his own honor, he must see to it that his law is respected and upheld. I.e., for God to be true to himself (i.e., righteous), he must make sure that either the law's COMMANDS are honored and obeyed, OR that the law's PENALTY is strictly applied and followed. When the commands of his law are violated by human sin, God's holy nature demands that the law's PENALTY be satisfied. Either way, God is righteous.

8. PERSONAL RIGHTEOUSNESS VS. GOD'S RIGHTEOUSNESS

In the previous chapter we spoke of human righteousness as well as God's righteousness. Distinguishing between them is very important as we try to understand grace, since we cannot be saved without righteousness.

First, what is "righteousness"? Basically, to be righteous means to be in conformity with the NORM by which one is properly and rightly measured. The proper norm to which human beings must conform is our Creator's law code. Thus we can define righteousness (especially in the context of grace) as "satisfying the requirements of the law." Mainly this includes satisfying the law's commands, but there is a sense in which it may include satisfying the law's penalty. These are two different ways one may be righteous in reference to one's law code.

Another way to say it is that to be righteous means to be "right with God," and this means especially to be right with God's law.

(A common current definition of righteousness is that it means "faithfulness to covenant promises." The idea is that Israel failed to live up to its covenant commitments, so Jesus came as a "stand-in" for

Israel and fulfilled Israel's covenant promises in its place. This, however, is woefully inadequate. Jesus did not come to "fix" Israel's failed relationship to its covenant; he came to resolve mankind's ruined relationship to God's law!)

We cannot maintain fellowship with God without righteousness. As Paul says in 1 Corinthians 6:9, "Do you not know that the unrighteous [lawbreakers] will not inherit the kingdom of God?" The norm to which we must conform in order to be righteous is our New Covenant law code. We must satisfy the commands of our law code to be accepted by God. The alternative, of course, is to be lawbreakers (sinners) and thus be condemned to satisfy the law's requirement for penalty. Since we are in fact sinners, our destiny would appear to be the latter. (This latter is actually a kind of righteousness—"being right with the law"—but not in a way that saves.)

But here is where the distinction between personal righteousness and God's righteousness comes to the rescue. PERSONAL righteousness is simply our OWN satisfaction of the requirements of God's law. We wish we could do this by means of our personal integrity, our faithfulness to God's will, our obedience to all law commands without any deviations. The problem here is seen in the message of Romans 1:18 – 3:20, "None is righteous, no, not one" (3:10); "for all have sinned and fall short of the glory of God" (3:23). As Isaiah 64:6 declares, "We have all become like one who is unclean, and all our righteous deeds are like a polluted garment."

What does this mean, then? Simply this: because we are sinners, we can no longer be right with God in terms of the law's *commands*, therefore the only alternative is to be right with God's law in terms of its *penalty*. Regarding our personal righteousness, we are doomed to be right with the law by suffering its penalty: eternity in hell.

Is there any hope for us? Not based on our own righteousness. But here is the point of the gospel of grace: God steps into our place and satisfies the requirements of the law FOR us! God makes sure that the requirements of his own law are satisfied. He does not allow his law to be besmirched or dishonored. He makes sure that the perfections of his law are upheld in absolute righteousness. And the glory of his grace is this: he GIVES that DIVINE righteousness—his OWN righteousness—to us as the basis for our salvation!

Going back to Isaiah, we will remember that in 64:6 he says that all our personal righteous deeds are like a filthy garment. But in 61:10, the prophet declares, "I will greatly rejoice in Yahweh; my soul shall exult in my God, for he has clothed me with the garments of salvation; he has covered me with the robe of [HIS!] righteousness." This gift of God's righteousness is the "righteousness of God" that Paul says is revealed in the gospel (Romans 1:16-17).

9. GOD'S RIGHTEOUSNESS: HIS PERFECT MORAL CHARACTER OR HIS GIFT TO SINNERS?

The Bible specifically says that we are saved by God's righteousness. For example, Paul says that the reason so many Jews were lost is that they were trying to be saved by their own righteousness, and thus did not submit themselves to God's righteousness (Romans 10:1-3). The gospel of salvation is so powerful because "in it the righteousness of God is revealed" (Romans 1:16-17).

This raises the question: when Paul speaks about "the righteousness of God," exactly what is he talking about? Here is where we must make another distinction: we must distinguish between God's righteousness as his PERFECT MORAL CHARACTER, and his righteousness as his GIFT TO SINNERS.

The point here is to understand exactly what is meant by GOD'S righteousness when it is involved in the salvation of sinners. Most of the time, when the Bible refers to the righteousness of God, it is talking about his perfectly consistent moral character, i.e., an attribute of his nature. But in the context of grace (e.g., Romans 1:16-17; 3:21-22; 5:18; 10:3-6) it seems to be something different, or at least something MORE. Failure to see this distinction can lead to much confusion about how we are saved.

Regarding the former, God's righteousness is in fact one of his main attributes. (See my book, "God the Redeemer," ch. 4, pp. 175-243.) Now, if righteousness means "conformity to a norm," does this mean God has a norm by which he must be measured? In a sense, yes. That "norm" is his own nature, the sum of his attributes. We can say it like this: the righteousness of God means that his actions will always be in perfect conformity to his nature or essence. Because the righteous God is holy, his actions can never violate his holiness. Because the righteous God is loving, his actions can never violate his love—and so on. He is self-consistent; he is eternally faithful to himself. This is his righteousness.

As we have seen, Paul says that the righteousness of God is part of the gospel (Romans 1:16-17), and "gospel" means "good news." But how is the righteousness of God GOOD NEWS to sinners? God must always be true to himself. That sounds good, as long as we are behaving ourselves. "God is love," so he will bless us. But the fact is that we are sinners, and God is also a "consuming fire" of wrath (Hebrews 12:29). So what can we sinners expect from a righteous God except hell? How is his righteousness "good news" to sinners?

Here is where we must learn to think of the righteousness of God as more than the simple inward attribute of his personal moral character. As the Bible presents it in the context of the gospel, God's righteousness is something separate from his own nature, something that can be wrapped up in a gift package and given (transferred, imputed) to sinners, like the "robe of righteousness" in Isaiah 61:10.

To understand this, we must think of the righteousness of God not just as something God IS, but as something God DOES. The righteous God DOES something that upholds the integrity of his law, and the effects of that act are then transferred (imputed) to us sinners and become the basis for our salvation. Thus we are saved not by our OWN righteousness, but by GOD'S righteousness.

What is this thing that God does, that constitutes his gift of righteousness to sinners? Here is where Jesus Christ comes into the picture. Jesus, as the incarnation of God the Son, "acted out" the righteousness of God in our history in the place of sinners. What Jesus did for us constitutes the righteousness of God that is the basis of our salvation. His righteousness is God's gracious gift to us.

10. LAW'S COMMANDS SATISFIED, OR LAW'S PENALTY SATISFIED?

The issue here is this: of all that Jesus did while he was on earth, exactly what part of that is transferred (imputed) to us as "the righteousness of God"? Here we must distinguish between Jesus's satisfaction of the law's COMMANDS, and his satisfaction of its PENALTY. We have described righteousness (as used in the context of grace) as satisfaction of the requirements of the law. We have said that God the Son as Jesus of Nazareth "acted out" this righteousness for us. I.e., he satisfied the requirements of the law for us, and this is given to us as a gift and counted as our own.

The question is, in what ways did Jesus "satisfy the requirements of the law," and how was this transferred to us? There is considerable confusion and misunderstanding here, so we must spell it out carefully.

Jesus satisfied the requirements of the law in two distinct ways. First, he was sinless, i.e., he perfectly obeyed all the COMMANDS of the law under which he lived as a human being (mainly the Law of Moses). This is called his active obedience or active righteousness. Many believe that this "righteousness of God" is transferred (imputed) to believing sinners as the basis for their justification before

God. Jesus's record of perfect obedience is transferred to our account, and God counts it as ours and considers us to be righteous. This is a very widespread belief.

This, however, is WRONG. For one thing, the perfect obedience of Jesus was no more than he, the man, already owed to God as a human being living under the law code of the Mosaic Law. He had nothing "left over," so to speak, to share with anyone else. (This is a conclusion based on Luke 17:7-10.) Even as a perfect human being Jesus was an "unprofitable servant."

Another reason why it is wrong to think that Jesus' perfect obedience is the "righteousness of God" imputed to sinners is that the Bible says (Romans 5:18) that "one act of righteousness leads to justification and life for all men." ONE ACT of righteousness! This would be not his perfect life, but his CRUCIFIXION, the one act in which Jesus was satisfying the requirement of the law FOR PENALTY for the entire human race! This is called Jesus's passive obedience or passive righteousness—and THIS IS ALL THE RIGHTEOUSNESS WE NEED for justification before God!

It is this passive righteousness alone that is the righteousness of God revealed in the gospel, and the righteousness of God that is imputed to sinners and on the basis of which God justifies us. Because Jesus on the cross submitted himself to the infinite wrath of God in our place, when this "one act" is applied to us, we are justified. The meaning of justification is this: God as Judge looks at us and declares, "No penalty for you!" (See Romans 8:1.) That is all we need for justification.

Jesus did indeed satisfy the law's commands perfectly, and also the law's eternal penalty. But he did the former for himself, to maintain his own righteousness. Then as a perfect man as well as the infinite God incarnate, he satisfied the law's eternal penalty in our place, as our substitute, thus enabling the righteous God to justify us while maintaining his own righteousness (Romans 3:26; 2 Corinthians 5:21).

SUMMARY: HOW TO BE RIGHT WITH GOD BY MEANS OF:

I. THE LAW SYSTEM

A. **Basis of "rightness":** *Personal* **righteousness**

B. **How is this righteousness** *achieved* **by us? Via obedience to LAW commands.**

   1. **Law commands = content of one's** *law code.*

   2. **One's response to law commands = "works of law"(in Paul).**

II. THE GRACE SYSTEM

A. **Basis of salvation:** *God's* **(i.e.,** *Christ's***) righteousness**

B. **How is this righteousness** *received* **by us? Via obedience to GOSPEL commands.**

   1. **Gospel commands = God's instructions on how to be saved.**

   2. **One's obedience to gospel commands = generic works = ("things we do").**

   3. **Even faith is a "work" in this generic sense. See John 6:26-29.**

PART TWO

GRACE ACCOMPLISHED AND APPLIED

1. GRACE ISN'T FAIR—BUT THAT'S GOOD!

Almost everyone develops a "fairness mentality" to some degree. We are conditioned from childhood to respect and seek fairness, otherwise known as justice. We know what it means to deserve (or not deserve) something. Very early in life, kids learn to say, "That's not fair!"

Most of the world, including many groups and individuals within Christendom, try to apply the fairness mentality to salvation itself. The assumption is that only those who are "good enough" go to heaven. Long ago I saw the results of some random answers to the question, "What are your chances of going to heaven?" One person said, "50-50. The older I get, the more I think my chances will improve." Another said, "My chances are kind of slim, maybe 50-50. You have to be more than a nice person. But I'm still in the running." An optimist said, "85%! I don't think the entrance exam will be that tough."

Like many others, all of these folks were obviously assuming that Judgment Day will involve something like a balance scale, where sins are on one side of the scale and good deeds on the other. One's good deeds must outweigh the bad, perhaps significantly. Only then will we *deserve* heaven.

The fact is this: the FAIRNESS approach to salvation is futile! James 2:10 says even *one sin* outweighs all the good we can do. The only way to deserve heaven is to be perfect: 100% good. Even 85% is not good enough, and 50% does not come close.

Here's the deal: when it comes to salvation, *forget about fairness!* If you want God to be fair with you on the Day of Judgment, you will go to hell. That's what all sinners *deserve.* If you really want to go to heaven, rather than fairness you must think instead in terms of GRACE. And we must get this through our heads: grace is the OPPOSITE of fairness! Grace means that on the Judgment Day, we will get the very opposite of what we deserve.

In most matters of this world, fairness is definitely a virtue. Children should be taught to be fair, to play fair, and to share fairly. We expect our courts of law to apply justice and fairness. We believe in an honest day's work for an honest day's pay.

But when it comes to eternal salvation, our only hope is grace—and grace is the very opposite of justice and fairness. Very often, even Christians have trouble accepting this. I heard a Bible college chapel speaker once say, "God will give to those who MERIT it, the blessings of eternal life." No! When it comes to salvation, we must STOP thinking in terms of merit or fairness, and think in terms of GRACE.

Our usual Sunday-school definition of grace is "unmerited favor." This is okay as far as it goes, but it does not go far enough! God's gift of salvation to a sinner is not just unmerited or undeserved; it is the *opposite* of what the sinner deserves! As one of my early seminary students put it, grace is "favor bestowed when wrath is owed."

Jesus's parable of the Pharisee and the tax collector (publican) teaches us the difference between the fairness mentality and the grace mentality (see Luke 18:9-14). First the Pharisee recites his list of good works and his supposed absence of sins (vv. 11-12), with the implicit assumption that he is obviously deserving of God's favor. Then the tax collector prays with the grace mentality. He did not say, "God, be fair with me, the sinner." He said, "God, be merciful to me, the sinner" (v. 13). Only the latter went home forgiven (justified), said Jesus (v. 14).

When you think of the Judgment Day, are you *afraid*, because you are thinking, "I know I'm not good enough to go to heaven"? STOP IT! Stop thinking like this! *Of course* you are not good enough! No one is! That's why God has given us GRACE, and that's why we must think in terms of grace!

We must be like the tax collector, and forget the balance-scales idea of Judgment Day. To go to heaven by the balance scale, you would have to live a perfect life. The only balance scale judgment that really works is this: all our sins go on one side of the scale, and Christ's atoning death goes on the other! Only his death can "outweigh" our sins, or "make up for" our sins. And no, that's not fair – IT'S GRACE!

2. NOT BY LAW

Think of heaven (just for the purpose of this illustration) as a gigantic city enclosed by an impenetrable and unscalable wall. You can see this city from afar, and you desperately want to enter into it. Your life is a journey toward it.

As you begin to get closer to this heavenly city, you can see that there are two gates that allow entry through the wall. Soon you can see that each gate has a large sign above it. Over one gate the sign says "LAW," and over the other the sign says "GRACE." And then you understand. Theoretically at least, there are two ways of getting into heaven: the LAW way, and the GRACE way. You can enter through the law gate, or through the grace gate.

You get a little closer to the city, and you see a large group of people lined up at each gate—and you are in one of those lines! Every human being, including yourself, is either in the law line, or in the grace line. What difference does it make? The fact is that it makes an eternal difference, as will now be explained.

When you get close enough to the heavenly city and its two gates, you can see that each gate has a sign posted on it, explaining the conditions for passing through that gate into heaven. The sign on the law gate says in big letters, "KEEP THE COMMANDMENTS; ESCAPE THE PENALTY. BREAK THE COMMANDMENTS; SUFFER THE PENALTY." What does this mean?

Here is the explanation. It means that every human being lives under a law code revealed by the Creator God. One's applicable law code is composed of commandments he or she is obligated to obey, and it also contains a penalty that will be applied if we break even one of these commandments (James 2:10; Galatians 3:10). The penalty is eternity in hell.

There are three main law codes; they apply as follows. All human beings, by virtue of being created in the image of God, have been equipped with an intuitive law code "written on the heart" (Romans 2:15); every person is obligated to live by this law code. Also, God gave the Israelite nation a special law code — the Mosaic Law — that applied to them from Sinai (Exodus 19) to Pentecost (Acts 2). By the Jews' calculation, this OT law code contained 613 commands. After Pentecost God gave new revelation (the New Testament) containing a different law code that now applies to all now living, including Christians. This New Covenant law code has over a thousand commands we are all now obligated to obey (in addition to the law written on the heart). These are the commandments to which the sign on the law gate refers.

So what does this sign mean? It means you can enter into heaven through the law gate IF you have kept ALL - 100% - of the commandments of the law code you are living under. If you have sinned even once, i.e., broken even one of these commandments, you must pay the penalty of eternity in hell. It's that simple: you can enter here (through the law gate) by keeping all the commands that apply to you — perfectly, all your life. You must have a lifetime of sinlessness or perfect obedience.

At this point the terrifying truth strikes us: though there is a law gate into heaven, *no one will actually enter heaven through it!* That is simply because no one meets the qualifications posted thereon. As Romans 3:23 sadly says, "All have sinned." Thus the law gate into heaven is closed, locked, and permanently sealed shut by the universality of sin. What makes this even sadder is the fact that so many human beings are actually lining up at this gate, futilely hoping to enter heaven thereby, because they are unaware that there is another gate — the one over which is written the word GRACE.

When we turn our attention to the grace gate, we see the sign posted on it, which explains the terms of entering heaven under the grace system. The grace sign says, in large letters, "KEEP THE COMMANDMENTS, BUT SUFFER THE PENALTY. BREAK THE COMMANDMENTS, BUT ESCAPE THE PENALTY." This startles us at first, because it seems so odd; in fact, it seems *unfair*. But then we remember that grace by nature is the opposite of fair. What exactly does it mean, then?

The grace formula means that you do not enter the grace gate into heaven based on the record of what YOU have done, but based on what Jesus Christ has done. You see, the first line of the formula — "Keep the commandments, but suffer the penalty" — does not apply to you or to any other sinner; it applies only to Jesus Christ.

Grace begins with Jesus. As a human being he kept his law-code commands perfectly (he was sinless), BUT he also suffered a penalty equivalent to eternity in hell in our place! The one who knew no sin was made to be sin on our behalf (2 Corinthians 5:21).

But that's not all. The second part of the grace formula DOES apply to us law-breakers who are in Jesus Christ: "Break the commandments, but escape the penalty." We have sinned, but God is not holding our sins against us! We enter heaven through the grace gate not because of our own righteousness, but because of Christ's righteousness (i.e., his payment of the law's penalty for us).

So here is the essence of grace. We are not under law; i.e., under the law system of salvation (Romans 6:14, 15). We are not in the law line, thinking we will enter the law gate into heaven. That is hopeless and futile anyway, since the law gate is sealed by sin and NO ONE will enter through it. But we do not despair. In fact, we rejoice, because we as believers are under grace, i.e., under the grace system of salvation. We are in the grace line, knowing we will enter the grace gate into heaven because of Jesus Christ.

3. DOUBLE CURSE, DOUBLE CURE

The English word "grace" can be used in three ways. First, it can refer to the *cause* of salvation: it represents the aspect of God's nature that causes him to love sinners and seek their salvation even though they do not deserve it. Second, "grace" can refer to the *way* of salvation: we are saved by the grace system (via the grace gate), as contrasted with the impotent law system (via the law gate).

The third way we use the word "grace" is this: it refers to the *content* of salvation, which we receive as a gift in the moment when we make the transition from lost to saved. In this sense grace is like a package we receive at conversion. What's in this package? An old hymn ("Rock of Ages") includes this prayer: "Be of sin the double cure: save me from its guilt and power." (Another version says, "Save from wrath and make me pure.") This "double cure" is the content of grace.

If grace is a double cure, then sin must inflict upon us a "double trouble" or a "double curse." Two of the worst curses in life are serious debt and serious sickness, which often fall upon someone together as the result of a catastrophic illness. This has happened to every man and woman in a spiritual sense as the result of sin. Every sinner is under a double curse. How do we explain this?

First, sin makes us *guilty*. When we break God's law, we become guilty sinners. This guilt puts us into debt to God: we OWE him the debt of eternal punishment in hell (Matthew 6:12: "Forgive us our debts"). This is the sinner's most serious problem. It is like a slave owing his master millions of dollars — an unimaginable and unpayable sum (see Matthew 18:23-35).

Second, sin gives the sinner a *sinful nature*. It is like having a fatal illness of the body, only in this case the disease of sin affects the soul (i.e., the spirit, heart, or inner man). Sin is not just an act; it is a *condition*, a state of sinfulness or corruption or depravity (partial, not total). As Jeremiah 17:9 says, "The heart is deceitful above all things, and desperately sick." It is even called a state of spiritual death (Ephesians 2:1, 5; Colossians 2:13).

If I wanted to write this "double curse" up for a national gossip magazine (like *The National Enquirer*), I would give it this catchy title for the cover: "Preacher Confesses: I'm in Trouble with the Law, and I Have a Bad Disease!"

But this is not where the narrative ends. It's time now for "the rest of the story," as Christian broadcaster Paul Harvey used to say. The whole purpose of God's grace is to counteract this double curse with a DOUBLE CURE! "Amazing grace" solves both aspects of the curse of sin.

First, to resolve the problem of guilt and punishment, God gives us the *forgiveness of sins*, or what the Bible often calls *justification*.

We are "justified freely by his grace" (Romans 3:24). God is "the justifier of the one who has faith in Jesus" (Romans 3:26). This means that our "lawless deeds are forgiven," and our "sins are covered" (Romans 4:7). It means that God is not holding our sins against us (Romans 4:8); he does not require us to pay him the debt we owe him, i.e., eternity in hell.

The reason the righteous God is able to do this is that he himself — in the second person of the Trinity, God the Son — became a human being and paid the debt for us! He took upon himself our penalty of God's eternal wrath when he died for us on the cross. Thus we are "justified by his blood" (Romans 5:9).

Justification thus means that in the moment of our conversion (i.e., our baptism), God's attitude toward us instantaneously changes from wrath to grace (he already loved us, of course). He no longer looks at us as guilty, hell-bound sinners, but as his forgiven children. "Justification" is literally a legal term. It means that God in his role as Judge looks at us as defendants, and he addresses this legal declaration to us: "No penalty for you!" (See Romans 8:1.) And he continues to whisper this in our spiritual ear for as long as we hold on to Jesus Christ as our Lord and Savior. Our debt of punishment is gone, because Jesus paid it for us.

But that is just the first part of the double cure. In the second place, the grace of God resolves the problem of our spiritual sickness and restores us to spiritual wholeness. Here God is working on us in his role of Healer or Physician; indeed, he is performing "open-heart surgery" upon our souls. He is giving us a spiritual heart transplant:

"And I will remove the heart of stone from your flesh and give you a heart of flesh" (Ezekiel 36:26).

This direct operation on the heart is usually called *regeneration* (see Titus 3:5), but it is the same as being "born again" (John 3:3, 5), and being raised up from spiritual death to new spiritual life (Ephesians 2:5-6; Colossians 2:12-13). It is also a "new creation" (2 Corinthians 5:17). It is the spiritual equivalent of what doctors in old western movies used to mean when they said, "The fever broke."

This moment of regeneration is caused by the renewing power of the gift of the indwelling Holy Spirit (Ezekiel 36:27; Acts 2:38; Titus 3:5; John 3:5). This instantaneous event is just the beginning of the life-long healing process usually called *sanctification,* which is empowered by the continuing indwelling of the Holy Spirit (Romans 8:13; Ephesians 3:16; 1 Thessalonians 5:23). The success of this process depends on our ongoing submission to and cooperation with the Spirit (Philippians 2:12-13).

So who are we now, or where do we stand now—now that we have received the double cure of grace? What is our Christian life all about? Two things: we are NOT in the process of trying to pay our debt to God, or trying to "make it up" to God, or trying to work off the consequences of our sins in some way. Justification means that "Jesus paid it all!" We are continuing to trust this promise. Also, we are in the process of getting well from a serious disease. This includes following the divine Doctor's instructions on how to live so as to help facilitate this healing.

What happens when we die and meet God face to face? We will no doubt still have a residue of sin in our lives; we will not be perfectly healed yet. But this does not disqualify us from heaven! This is when God will make us completely well in our spirits; this is when our spirits will be "made perfect" (Hebrews 12:23). The main point, though, is this: when we die and meet God, in the most important way we will still be the same as we are now! We will meet God *100% debt free!* There will be nothing to pay – no penalty for us – EVER! This is the "blessed assurance" that grace gives us.

4. THROUGH JESUS CHRIST

Romans 3:24-25 says, "We are all justified freely by his grace through the redemption that is in Christ Jesus, whom God set forth to be a propitiation — a sacrifice of atonement — through faith in his blood" (composite translation).

The only way to be saved from sin is by grace, and the only source of grace is what Jesus has done for us on the cross. Here we are seeking to understand exactly what Jesus was doing on the cross to make salvation by grace possible.

I. GRACE COMES BY JESUS CHRIST.

The general or generic meaning of the Greek word for grace (*charis*) is "a gift that brings joy," so both *charis* and our English word "grace" can refer to gifts of different kinds. But the Bible is very clear that *saving* grace comes through Jesus Christ alone. "Grace and truth were realized through Jesus Christ" (John 1:17). "Be strong in the grace that is in Jesus Christ" (2 Timothy 2:1). "We are saved through the grace of the Lord Jesus" (Acts 15:11). "For the grace of God has appeared, bringing salvation to all men" (Titus 2:11). See Romans 3:24; 5:15.

We must stress that Jesus is the ONLY source of saving grace. "And there is salvation in no one else; for there is no other name under heaven that has been given among men by which we must be saved" (Acts 4:12). Most religions have a concept of "salvation," but none of them can truly save. This is because sinners can be saved only by grace, and grace comes only through Jesus. Sects such as *bhakti* Hinduism and True Pure Land Buddhism CLAIM to provide a gracious salvation, but they are deceiving themselves and others. Grace is possible nowhere outside Christianity, because Christianity alone has the only true source of grace: the sinless divine Redeemer, Jesus Christ.

II. GRACE COMES BY THE CROSS OF JESUS CHRIST.

Why is Jesus different from other so-called "saviors," such as some Buddha, or Krishna, or Mohammed, or Sun Moon, or Joseph Smith? What is there about Jesus that makes him the sole source of grace? Two things:

First, Jesus brings grace because of *who he is*. For one thing, he is the only *sinless* human being, and only a sinless human being can offer himself to suffer the penalty for sin deserved by someone else. For another thing, he alone is the divine Son of God, God the Son, God in the flesh. Only a divine being can offer himself to suffer the penalty for sin deserved by the whole world.

Second, Jesus brings grace because of *what he has done*. Remember: grace is not fair; it is even the opposite of fair. Under grace one does not get what he deserves, but rather its opposite. This is just as true of Jesus as it is of us. What did Christ deserve? The highest praise and honor; see Revelation 5:11-14. But what did he get? He got the CROSS! *He* did not deserve the cross, but we did! He was taking what WE deserve so that he can give us what HE deserves. See 2 Corinthians 5:21.

How does the Bible describe what Jesus was doing on the cross? Here I will stress two things. First, the cross was our REDEMPTION (see Romans 3:24). "To redeem" means to set free by paying a price, or in this case, by paying a DEBT that we owe. Sin puts us in debt to God (Matthew 6:12). We are under bondage or obligation to pay God the debt of eternal punishment in hell. Jesus *redeems* us by paying this debt for us. In his suffering, Jesus was experiencing the equivalent of eternity in hell for all mankind. He thus sets us free from the obligation of paying this debt. See Galatians 3:13; 1 Peter 1:18-19.

Second, the cross was our PROPITIATION (Romans 3:25). "To propitiate" means to turn away wrath by an offering. Because of our sin, we deserve God's wrath and are justly condemned to suffer the consequences of this wrath for all eternity. But Jesus intervenes for us, and takes the wrath of God (which WE deserve) upon HIMSELF instead. He put himself in our place and allowed the Father to pour out his divine wrath upon him. This is how he is our propitiation. See 1 John 2:2; 4:10.

We cannot begin to understand what Jesus was going through on the cross. The physical torture of crucifixion was extreme in itself. But the *spiritual* (mental, emotional) suffering which accompanied

Christ's crucifixion was infinitely worse, given the fact that he was the sinless Son of God.

The cross of Christ, and his cross ALONE, allows God to be both just and the justifier of whoever trusts in him. See Romans 3:26.

III. GRACE COMES *BY FAITH* IN THE CROSS OF JESUS CHRIST.

The cross of Jesus Christ does not provide salvation for all sins automatically for all mankind. True, it automatically cancels out the consequences of *Adam's* sin for everyone (Romans 5:12-19), but our own personal, conscious sins will be forgiven only when we consciously accept Christ's gift of redemption. Romans 3:25 (correctly translated, as in the NIV) declares that Christ is a propitiation "through FAITH in his BLOOD." Saving faith must be this specific. See also Romans 10:9-10.

The benefits of Christ's propitiation are first applied to the sinner in Christian baptism, but only through faith. See Romans 6:3-4; Colossians 2:12. We as Christians are acceptable to God NOW, at this very moment, not because of how good we are, but because we are still trusting in Jesus's blood.

Why is this the only way? Actually, human pride would LIKE to think there could be another way besides grace, a way in which we could be seen as somehow deserving of salvation. *But the cross will not allow it!* Whenever you begin to think that you might deserve to be saved, just take another look at the cross: that's what you deserve! "When I survey the wondrous cross, on which the Prince of Glory died, my richest gain I count but loss, and pour contempt on all my pride." See Ephesians 2:9; James 4:6.

5. JUSTIFIED BY FAITH: THE KEY TO ASSURANCE

The immediate practical benefit of understanding that we are saved by grace is that we have assurance of salvation. Assurance is not the same as "once saved, always saved." It is a confidence in our present security in Jesus Christ. Ask yourself the question, "If I were to die right now, or Jesus were to return right now, would I be saved?" *Assurance* is being able to say "YES!" to this question, and every Christian should be able to do this, because of grace.

The problem is that many Christians do not have this assurance, because they do not understand what it means to be saved by grace. Even as they sing the old hymn, "Blessed assurance, Jesus is mine!," in their hearts they are thinking, "Maybe — I hope so — I'm not really sure!"

In this lesson we are trying to help these doubters get over their uncertainty. There is a specific way to do this. When I teach my seminary course on grace, on the first day of class I tell the students that I can sum up the whole course in one sentence: "A right understanding of *justification by faith* is the key to assurance of salvation." Let's see how this works.

ONE: There is just one way to know you are saved, and that is to know you ARE JUSTIFIED. As Paul says in Romans 5:1-2, "Therefore, having been justified by faith, we have peace with God through our Lord Jesus Christ, through whom also we have obtained our introduction by faith into this grace in which we stand; and we exult in hope of the glory of God."

In Lesson 3 above we explained the meaning of justification. It is the same as having the debt of penalty for your sins forgiven. It is a legal term. It refers to standing before the Judge of the universe in the divine courtroom and having him declare, "NO PENALTY FOR YOU!" This happens not only on the future Judgment Day. It is happening now, and will be happening throughout our lives as believers. This is why we have assurance of salvation. We know we are justified; we know our sins are forgiven. It is not a question of how good we are, but how forgiven we are. It is hearing God say, "No penalty for you! No condemnation for you (Romans 8:1)! No hell for you! No fear for you!"

The next question is this: exactly what is the basis for this confidence?

TWO. There is just one way for a sinner to be justified, and that is BY THE BLOOD OF CHRIST. As Paul says in Romans 5:9, we have "been justified by His blood."

Actually, theoretically, there is another way one might be justified, namely, by the law system. Under law we could hear the Judge say, "No penalty for you" — if we have never sinned. A totally innocent person would be justified because he is 100% good.

But in fact this will not work for us, because we have all sinned and come short of God's glory (Romans 3:23). We are sinners. The question then is: can God justify *even a sinner*? The answer is YES! See Romans 4:5: God justifies even the ungodly! This is the amazing thing about grace!

But on what basis can God justify sinners — forgive their penalty — when they actually deserve eternal punishment in hell? Because under grace God does not treat us as we deserve. Under grace we are not justified by our works (by being 100% good), but by grace — because we are 100% forgiven by the blood of Jesus Christ (Romans 3:24; 5:9).

Under grace, regarding the question, "Are you saved?", the answer depends not on how good you are but on how powerful and efficacious the blood of Christ is. In lesson 4 above, we saw the answer to this question. We saw that Jesus' death on the cross was a work of redemption, and a work of propitiation. Because of his sinless and divine nature, Jesus suffered the equivalent of eternity in hell for the whole human race. He has already paid the penalty for our sins.

So if we are under the blood of Jesus Christ, our sins are covered; they are in a sense "hidden" from God's sight (Romans 4:6-8). When God looks at us, our sins are hidden from his sight in the sense that he does not count them against us (2 Corinthians 5:19). Thus he can say, "NO PENALTY FOR YOU!" He can treat me *"just if I'd"* [justified!] already spent eternity in hell and paid my penalty. [He does NOT treat me *"just if I'd"* never sinned."]

This leaves one more step in our quest for assurance:

THREE. There is just one way to be under the blood of Christ, and that is BY FAITH. As Paul says in Romans 3:28, "For we maintain that a man is justified by faith apart from works of the Law." That is why he says in Romans 5:1, "Having been justified BY FAITH, we have peace with God."

Justifying faith includes two elements. One is called *assent*, because it is an act of the MIND as it gives assent to the truth of specific statements about Jesus and his salvation. It is what the Bible describes as "believing THAT" certain things are true. For example, John 20:31 says God has given you the testimony of Scripture "so that you may BELIEVE THAT Jesus is the Christ, the Son of God; and that believing you may have life in His name." Also, Romans 10:9 says that if you "BELIEVE in your heart THAT God raised Him from the dead, you will be saved."

The other aspect of faith is called *trust*, because it is an act of the WILL as directed toward the person of Jesus Christ. In Biblical language, this trust is called "believing IN" and "believing ON" Jesus (e.g., John 3:16; Acts 16:31). It means entrusting our very eternal existence into Jesus' hands, the way one trusts his health into a doctor's care or her children into the hands of a babysitter.

To be justified by faith means that this faith in the saving works of Jesus (rather than faith in the worthiness of our own works) is the connection point in our lives into which the power line of justification is plugged. This is true in two steps.

First, we BEGIN to be justified BY FAITH, when we initially come under the blood of Christ in baptism. The Bible is clear that this connection with the blood of Christ begins in the moment of baptism (Acts 2:38; 22:16; Romans 6:3-4; Colossians 2:12). But baptism is just the TIME we were first justified (forgiven), not the MEANS by which the justification is received. As Colossians 2:12 says, we were united with Christ "in baptism," as the time; but it was "by faith" as the means. (Note: "by faith" is not the same as "as soon as you have faith.") Even in baptism, what God is looking for is the faith in the sinner's heart.

The second step is that, after baptism, we CONTINUE to be justified BY FAITH. We initially became justified by faith (in baptism), and we STAY justified by faith. We continue to live in a forgiven state, not because we do not sin, but because we are constantly trusting in the sin-covering blood of Jesus Christ. Failure to understand this point is a main reason why many lack assurance. I will discuss this further in the next lesson.

6. GRACE VS. GALATIANISM

In lesson five I said that many Christians lack assurance of salvation because they do not understand how "justification by faith" relates to STAYING saved, once one has become a Christian. It is important to distinguish between these two questions: (1) How does a sinner BECOME saved? and (2) How does a Christian STAY saved?

Many Christians, especially in the Restoration Movement, know how to answer the first question; but many are seriously confused about the second one. A common but faulty approach to this issue is often called *Galatianism*. It is called this because it is the false view of salvation that Paul is refuting in his letter to the Galatians. This false view—Galatianism—is summarized thus: a sinner *becomes* saved by grace, but *stays* saved by works.

An example of this view is someone whom many of us admire for many reasons, namely, Alexander Campbell. In a letter to "Paulinus" in 1827 he specifically said, "Sinners are justified by faith, and Christians by works." He explained that in the final judgment, faith will not be accounted to anyone for righteousness; "every Christian will be justified by his works. Nothing else comes in review on the day of judgment" (*The Christian Baptist*, IV:10).

Such a view, like all versions of Galatianism, must be rejected as a denial of the Biblical teaching on justification by faith and thus as a denial of grace. To say we are justified by faith is not just a one-time event occurring at the beginning of our Christian life, but is an on-going state that keeps us saved in spite of our sins.

Unfortunately this Galatianist view has been accepted by many, especially in the Restoration Movement. Why have we been so vulnerable to it? Because several other of our favorite doctrines—also questionable—contribute to it. I will briefly explain three of them.

I.   THE "FIVE-FINGER" SALVATION PLAN.

The Restoration Movement has had many versions of the five-point "plan of salvation," some more Galatianist than others. A common one is that a person is saved by believing, repenting, confessing, being baptized, and living the Christian life. The problem with this is that it is usually presented as if all five of these actions are equally significant in "achieving" salvation. For example, we often see them illustrated as five equal steps in a staircase leading to eternal life.

Where we go wrong here is in the implication that the fifth step, "living the Christian life," has the same significance for salvation as the other four. This is simply not the case; it is a perfect example of Galatianism. As often presented, in the first four steps we describe the way to BECOME saved, and the fifth step (living the Christian life) is explained as the way to STAY saved. We stay saved, then, by our works. Thus in our presentation of the plan we switch gears, changing from grace to law after the fourth step; and we thereby implant the notion of works-salvation in the convert's heart from the very beginning of his or her Christian life.

If we are still going to use this five-step plan, the fifth step must be explained as qualitatively different from the others. Steps one through four are the essence of obeying the gospel, whereas "living the Christian life" is the essence of obeying our law code (i.e., it is "works of law). We should still stress faith, repentance, confession, and baptism as gospel or grace commands, and as the Biblical conditions for *becoming* saved (justified and born again). But we should stress that ongoing faith, repentance, and confession are the continuing conditions for *staying* saved. We should also make it clear that living the Christian life is the expected and consistent result of these things (a la Romans 6).

II. BAPTISM FOR THE FORGIVENESS OF PAST SINS ONLY.

Another false doctrine that opens the door to Galatianism is an old one, having arisen in the second century A.D. It is the belief that baptism does bring forgiveness of sins, but ONLY for the sins one has committed up to that point. This is a serious error, and it leads to all kinds of works-oriented attempts to deal with sins committed after the baptismal moment.

The earliest approach (later second century) was that there simply is NO forgiveness for post-baptismal sins. At the beginning of the third century, some (e.g., Tertullian) began to teach that God will accept *one more* episode of repentance, but it must be quite a sensational display. Ultimately the Roman Catholic Church, still believing that only past sins are forgiven in baptism, created the sacrament of penance (today, called reconciliation) as the way of dealing with post-baptismal sins.

This concept has not died out. The idea that in baptism one receives forgiveness only for sins previously committed is still present, especially in the Restoration Movement. A recent testimony in one of our Christian magazines, by a Restoration stalwart, said: "When I accepted and obeyed Christ, I was saved from my past sins." My farming background has led me to call this "sheep-dip baptism." For non-farmers we can call it "car-wash baptism." All the dirt from the past is washed away. Now what do we do if (or rather, *when*) we sin again? Trying to answer this question almost always leads to a form of Galatianism. (See the next point.)

We can avoid this problem by seeing that baptism is for the forgiveness of sins, *period.* In baptism we enter a saving relationship with Jesus Christ. This relationship keeps us in the forgiven state. In baptism we are covered with the robe of Christ's righteousness (Isaiah 61:10), which covers our filthy rags (Isaiah 64:6). Even though we are still sinners, we are *forgiven* sinners.

III. A WRONG UNDERSTANDING OF 1 JOHN 1:9.

In the Restoration Movement one of the most common roadblocks to assurance, and a common cause of Galatianism, is a faulty understanding of 1 John 1:9, which says, "If we confess our sins, He is faithful and righteous to forgive us our sins and to cleanse us from all unrighteousness." Assuming that baptism is for the forgiveness of past sins only, many have taken this verse to be the key to obtaining forgiveness for sins committed after baptism.

The result is a ritualized mini-penance. It goes like this: after having our slate wiped clean in baptism, it is assumed that every time we sin we literally fall from grace and become lost again. The only way to be forgiven of that sin and to become saved again is to repent for and confess that specific sin, and pray for its forgiveness. Thus a person is trapped in a revolving door, an endless cycle of saved/sin/lost/confession/saved/sin/lost/confession/saved, etc. This causes a person to live in fear that he or she will die while in the "lost" phase of the cycle. This is clearly an example of "staying saved by works."

The error here is a failure to understand what it means to be justified by faith, apart from works of law (Romans 3:28). It means we stay under the forgiving blood of Christ by continuing to trust in his redemptive works, not by how well we keep our law code (sinning or not). We wear his righteousness to cover up our unrighteousness. We live in a forgiven (justified) state, as long as we are sincerely trusting in Jesus as our Savior.

So what does 1 John 1:9 mean? It is not talking about the specific confession of specific sins as the condition for the forgiveness of those sins. The context (vv. 8, 10) shows that John is saying that we must have a constant realization and ongoing confession *THAT we are sinners.* We must never get to the point where we think that we are no longer sinners, like the Pharisee in Jesus' parable (Luke 18:9-14). We must be like the tax collector, who confessed no specific sins, but simply acknowledged THAT he was a sinner in need of God's mercy. This is the man who went home forgiven, said Jesus.

(Confession of specific sins is part of the sanctification process, rather than a condition for justification.)

In conclusion, we must see that to continually trust in Jesus' blood is to REST the burden of our sin and guilt upon him, as many of our old hymns say. E.g., "Resting in my Savior as my all in all, I'm standing on the promises of God." This is a rest from *worry*, not a rest from *work* (see Romans 6:1ff.; Galatians 5:6; James 2:18ff.). When we are under Christ's blood, it is not just our sins that are forgiven, but WE OURSELVES are FORGIVEN PERSONS.

Assurance of salvation depends on being free from the GUILT of sin, even though we are not yet free from sin itself. We want to be, and some day will be, free from both; but while we are working on the sin, God has already taken away the guilt and punishment through Jesus' blood. We are not yet 100% good, but we are 100% forgiven. The latter is the basis of our assurance.

7. JUSTIFIED BY FAITH, YET JUDGED BY WORKS?

We have stressed, as does Paul, that sinners are justified by faith, apart from works of law (Romans 3:28; 5:1). But the fact is that many Biblical texts specifically say, or at least imply, that we will all somehow be JUDGED BY WORKS. See for example 2 Chronicles 6:30; Job 34:11; Proverbs 24:12; Ecclesiastes 12:13-14; Jeremiah 32:19; Ezekiel 33:20; Matthew 12:37; 25:31 ff.; Acts 10:34-35; Romans 14:12; 1 Corinthians 3:13; Ephesians 6:8; Colossians 3:25; James 2:18-26; Revelation 2:23; 20:12-13.

In addition to these, here are some I will quote: Psalm 62:12, "For You recompense a man according to his work." Isaiah 59:18, "According to their deeds, so He will repay." Jeremiah 17:10, "I, the LORD, search the heart, I test the mind, even to give to each man according to his ways, according to the results of his deeds." Matthew 16:27, at his second coming, Jesus "will then repay every man according to his deeds." Romans 2:6, God "will render to each person according to his deeds." 2 Corinthians 5:10, "For we must all appear before the judgment seat of Christ, so that each one may be recompensed for his deeds in the body, according to what he has done, whether good or bad." 1 Peter 1:17, God "impartially judges according to each one's work." Revelation 22:12, "Behold, I am coming quickly, and My reward is with Me, to render to every man according to what he has done."

How can we reconcile the teaching that we are justified by faith and not by works, with this abundant testimony that we will be judged by works?

I. FALSE ANSWERS TO THIS QUESTION

One false answer to the question is that when Paul speaks of being justified by faith and not by works, by "works" he is referring to the Law of Moses only. This cannot be the case, though, since Paul's use of the word "law," in the crucial passage of Romans 1-5, is not limited to the Mosaic Law. Here he discusses law as it applies to Gentiles (e.g., 1:18-32; 2:14-15), and as it applies to Abraham (e.g., 4:1-5). The non-justifying "works of law" (Romans 3:20, 28) include everyone's responses to whatever law code he or she may be under.

Another false answer is the idea that the faith that justifies actually INCLUDES works as part of its very definition. Works are just a part of faith; thus to be judged by works IS to be judged by faith. This claim, however, is simply not so. It is based on a faulty assumption regarding lexical definitions, namely, that if the words for faith (e.g., *pistis*) according to some (not all) Greek lexicons sometimes means "works," then whenever these words are used they must always include the connotation of works. This simply is not the way lexicons and lexical definitions work.

Another false answer is the Galatianism discussed in lesson six above, that we are indeed *initially* (at conversion) justified by faith;

but once we become Christians we *stay* justified by works and are finally judged only by our works. We have already seen, however, that this view is contrary to the very essence of justification by faith.

II. HOW THEN *CAN* WE EXPLAIN THE "JUDGED BY WORKS" TEXTS?

There are definitely some valid senses in which human beings are judged by works, even though our final destinies are determined by our faith-relationship to Jesus Christ. Here I will summarize a few of them.

First of all, in the OT, sometimes the judgment of which the writers speak is not eternal judgment but earthly judgment, e.g., rewarding Israel for covenant faithfulness or pouring out wrath upon Israel's enemies (e.g., 2 Chronicles 6:28-31; Isaiah 59:18).

Secondly, in the final judgment an examination of works is necessary to determine the DEGREE of rewards for individual believers. It seems there are degrees of punishment for the lost (Matthew 10:15; 11:22-24; Luke 10:12; 12:47-48; 20:47; John 19:11). Likewise the quantity and quality of believers' works will determine the degree of their rewards (e.g., Matthew 5:19; 18:4; Luke 19:12-19; James 3:1). This is especially evident in 1 Corinthians 3:12-15, which says the fire of judgment "will test the quality of each man's work." Some believers will be rewarded, and some not. This also seems to be the point of 2 Corinthians 5:10, which says that every believer will be recompensed for deeds done in this life, good and bad.

A third way works will enter into the final judgment is that they will be cited as EVIDENCE of the presence of faith. Justification is indeed by faith, but the faith that justifies is a faith that WORKS (Romans 1:5; James 2:14-26). Works thus demonstrate the state of the heart, just as a tree is known by its fruit (Matthew 12:33). The fruit does not determine the kind of tree, but demonstrates it. Likewise our works are the evidence of the presence of faith: John 15:1-8; Galatians 5:6; Ephesians 2:10; 1 Thessalonians 1:3; James 2:17-18.

One may wonder why it is necessary to survey the works of any individual in the judgment process since the omniscient God already knows who truly has faith and who does not. This is in fact true; God himself does not need to review our works in order to know if faith is present. But the point of the review is not for God's sake, but for the sake of others. The point of judgment by works is to demonstrate before all that God's judgment is impartial, that he is no "respecter of persons" (Acts 10:34-35; Romans 2:11; Ephesians 6:8-9; Colossians 3:25; 1 Peter 1:17). Judgment according to works thus demonstrates to all observers that God's judgment is completely in accord with his word, that he is showing no favoritism or partiality.

Finally, judgment according to works is only one part of the final judgment. In fact, it is a preliminary process, and in itself it does not yield a final result. It is immediately followed by a second stage of judgment, which is the deciding factor of where each of us will spend eternity. We see this in Revelation 20:11-15, which pictures two stages of judgment.

First, the BOOKS are opened, and every person is "judged from the things which were written in the books, according to their deeds"

(v. 12). These "books" are either the books of God's LAW (the law codes by which all will be judged), or the books that have recorded all of our deeds. The implication is that NO ONE is judged to be worthy of heaven based on what is written in the books, plural. But the final decision is not yet made.

The second and final phase of the judgment is then recorded in verse 15: "And if anyone's name was not found written in the BOOK OF LIFE, he was thrown into the lake of fire." What does this tell us? It tells us that our final destiny is not determined by what is written in the BOOKS, from which our works are judged. Rather, our final destiny is determined by whether our name is written in the BOOK, the book of life, "the book of life of the Lamb who has been slain" (Revelation 13:8). Only those who are trusting in Jesus' blood will pass this final test, and only because they are trusting in Jesus.

If we know, going into the judgment, that we are saved (and this is the point of assurance), and if God knows, going into the judgment, who is saved and who is not, what is the point of having all of us, especially believers, go through this uncomfortable (to say the least) judgment of works, even our sinful works, according to the books? Here is a suggestion. As a result of this full disclosure and remembrance of our works at the very threshold of heaven, it will be made perfectly plain that the ONLY reason we are saved for eternity is because of God's infinite grace and mercy. God's own mercy is thereby glorified, and we will enter heaven with hearts that are overflowing with humility, gratitude, and praise to the Redeemer.

8. SAVED BY GRACE, SAVED IN BAPTISM

We are now ready to explain how baptism and grace are related. First, I will state several basic principles to keep in mind when studying baptism. (A) Every doctrine, including baptism, is based on Scripture first, not on experience. (B) We cannot draw our conclusions about the meaning of baptism from non-Biblical sources, such as the Latin word *sacramentum* (which often meant "oath, pledge, covenant"). (C) Christian baptism began on the Day of Pentecost. Thus we must not try to base our understanding of it on pre-Pentecostal practices, such as OT circumcision or John's baptism. (D) There is only ONE BAPTISM, says Ephesians 4:5. Holy Spirit baptism and water baptism both apply to Christians, but they are not two separate events. They are the spiritual and the physical sides of a single baptismal event.

Finally, (E) Salvation as such is conditional, i.e., we receive salvation by meeting certain conditions. However, there are different KINDS of conditions. The main condition is faith, which is the sole MEANS (instrument, vehicle) by which the double cure of salvation is received: "By grace you have been saved *through faith*" (Ephesians 2:8). Baptism, on the other hand, is not just another condition for salvation, but another KIND of condition. Specifically, it is the TIME or occasion when God has said he will bestow grace upon the sinner; it is not the means of receiving salvation in the sense that faith is. Both faith and baptism are conditions for salvation, but faith is the means and baptism is the time. Please take care: do not equate condition with means, and do not confuse means and time.

Now we will briefly explore five basic NT texts that explain the meaning of baptism. For a fuller discussion of these and seven other such texts, see my book, *Baptism: A Biblical Study* (College Press, 2 ed., 2006).

ONE. MATTHEW 28:19-20. Four actions are specified in this Great Commission. The one main command is "Make disciples," an action that is preceded by the aorist (past) participle, "having gone." The means of making disciples is explained in two present participles: "baptizing them," and "teaching them." This activity began about ten days after this, on the Day of Pentecost (Acts 2:38-42).

It is very important that Jesus has separated baptism from teaching. Baptism is set apart because it is one of the conditions for *becoming* a Christian, along with the conditions of faith, repentance, and confession. Baptism alone is mentioned here, because it is the only one of these four things that those carrying out the Great Commission (apostles, evangelists) can do; the others are done by the converts. The doing of these things constitutes what the Bible calls obeying the gospel (Romans 10:16; 2 Thessalonians 1:8; 1 Peter 4:17). Then follows the second part of making disciples, i.e., teaching them to obey all that has been commanded. This refers to what Paul calls "works of law" (Romans 3:20, 28; Galatians 2:16), or the "good works" of obedience to one's law code, or living the Christian life. Many think baptism belongs in this second category, but Jesus has clearly set it apart from this one.

In his instruction to baptize, Jesus specifically says that sinners are to be baptized "into the name [*eis to onoma*] of the Father and of the Son and of the Holy Spirit." This tells us much about the meaning of baptism. The phrase "into the name of" in Greek culture was a technical business term used to indicate the entry of a sum of money or a piece of property into the account bearing the name of its owner. As Jesus uses it here, he means that this act of baptism is the time when one enters into an *ownership relation* with the persons of the Trinity. Here we become God's property, or slave (see Romans 6:15-23). From this point on we are seeking to fulfill our debt of obedience to our law code.

TWO. ACTS 2:38. This next text is set in the context of the beginning of the church, of the church age, of the New Covenant era. Peter has just preached the first gospel sermon (Acts 2:14-36), and his Jewish audience has come under deep conviction and is asking how to be set free from the guilt of their sin (2:37), which indicates that they had begun to believe the gospel. Peter instructs them to do two things: repent and be baptized. This audience would know what repentance is; this was a main part of the message of the OT prophets. They would also be familiar with a kind of baptism, given the ministry of John the Baptist. This baptism which Peter commands, however, was something new. Some in the audience had no doubt been baptized by John, but Peter said "each of you" must now receive Christian baptism. John's baptism was not enough (see Acts 19:1-7).

What did Peter say will be the result of this new baptism? Two things, corresponding to the double cure of grace. One is forgiveness of sins, which is the same as justification, or hearing God the Judge declare, "No penalty for you!" The second is the gift of the Holy Spirit, which is the new way the Holy Spirit is present within believers, the way John and Jesus called being "baptized with the Holy Spirit" (Acts 1:5). "Baptism in the Spirit" does NOT refer to the gift of tongues (Acts 2:1ff.); it is equivalent to what the Bible calls the indwelling of the Spirit (Romans 8:9-11), which is the source of the event called regeneration and of the ongoing process called sanctification.

In this text repentance and baptism cannot be separated; they are equal conditions for receiving the double cure of grace. Also, forgiveness and the indwelling of the Spirit cannot be separated. They are the two-fold essence of the saving grace received in baptism.

THREE. ROMANS 6:1-6. The context of this text also is very important. In Romans 1-5 Paul has just explained the BEST thing that has ever happened to us as Christians: we have been justified by faith in the redemptive works of Jesus, rather than by how well we have been able to respond to the commands of our law code (Romans 3:28). This is part one of the double cure. Now, in Romans 6:1ff., the Apostle is explaining the SECOND best thing that has happened to us, namely, the second part of the double cure: we have undergone an inward spiritual change so radical that it can be described as no less than a death and a resurrection to new life. Why is this latter change so wonderful? Because it makes it possible for us to live a holy life, i.e., to obey all that Jesus has commanded us (Matthew 28:20)!

So how does Paul bring baptism into the discussion? He gently chastises the Romans for their ignorance of these important events: "Don't you know what happened to you when you were baptized?" he asks (v. 3). In his explanation, he declares that one is *baptized into Christ*, i.e., into a union with Christ in his role as Redeemer. Specifically, one is *baptized into His death*, i.e., *we have been buried with Him through baptism into death*; and we are likewise united with him in his resurrection. This experience of salvation is unequivocally a result of being baptized.

Let us not yield to the temptation to blur the saving significance of baptism so clearly stated here. Note: Paul does not say we *repented* into Christ. He does not say we were buried with him through *faith* into death. The reference is to baptism. And let us not insult God by ignoring Ephesians 4:5 and saying (as one of my Calvinist professors at Westminster Seminary said), "There's not a drop of water in Romans six!" That goes for the next text as well.

FOUR. COLOSSIANS 2:11-13. This text is similar to Romans 6 in that it speaks of the spiritual change in our hearts as being comparable to a death and a resurrection, a change made possible by our coming into union with Jesus Christ. Here Paul says that in that moment we were "buried with Him" and "also raised up with Him." "He made you alive together with Him, having forgiven us all our transgressions"! But exactly when did this wonderful "regeneration and renewing" (see Titus 3:5) take place? Here Paul says it more clearly than anywhere else in the NT. He says it happens "IN BAPTISM," also adding the relative pronoun phrase, "IN WHICH."

It is significant that in this same verse (v. 12) Paul uses both the phrase "in baptism" and the phrase "through faith." We are buried and raised with him *in baptism,* but at the same time it is *through faith.* There is no paradox, no contradiction here. Baptism as the TIME of salvation is perfectly consistent with faith as the MEANS of receiving that salvation.

FIVE. 1 PETER 3:20-21. It is appropriate to close this brief study with Peter's statement that, just as the water of The Flood saved Noah's family by floating the ark, so also "baptism now saves you." Let us be clear: the water of The Flood is the symbolic analogy; baptism is the REALITY. Peter does not say baptism is "symbolizing" anything. Rather, baptism is DOING something: it SAVES.

Peter does make it clear that this salvation is not being accomplished through the physical effects of the water, but through the sinner's appeal or prayer to God for a good conscience. This is an indication of the sinner's faith and repentance, in answer to which God bestows forgiveness and clears the sinner's slate. But Peter goes even further to make it clear that the salvation given in baptism is not based on anything the sinner does. It happens only through the power of the redemptive work—the resurrection, in this case—of Jesus Christ.

These and other texts show that the Bible clearly teaches that we are saved by grace, but saved in baptism.

9. IS BAPTISM A WORK?

Many in the Christian world will vehemently reject just about everything I said in the previous lesson ("Saved by Grace, Saved in Baptism"). This is because they view baptism as a work, and believe that this automatically prevents baptism from having anything to do with salvation, since salvation is by grace. In this lesson I will show why this is false thinking.

Historically, for its first 1,500 years Christendom was nearly unanimous in its belief that water baptism is the moment of time when God initially bestows saving grace upon the sinner. This includes Martin Luther, who forcefully taught this view. He said, for example, that one is baptized so that he "may receive in the water the promised salvation" ("The Large Catechism," IV.36). Luther saw no conflict between baptism for salvation and salvation by grace.

The Copernican Revolution regarding the meaning of baptism came with the Swiss Reformer, Huldreich Zwingli. In the years 1523-1525 Zwingli completely reworked the doctrine of baptism. He repudiated any connection between baptism and salvation, and invented a totally new approach to it. In essence, he declared that baptism is the exact NT equivalent to OT circumcision, and is thus just a sign of an already-existing membership in God's covenant people. Zwingli of course knew this was a new view. He declared that "everyone before me has been wrong about baptism." Most Protestants have adopted this new view; many have done so without being aware of its relatively recent origin.

Those Protestants today who reject baptism as a salvation event follow Zwingli on this: they believe that such a view contradicts salvation by grace. The argument is this: Premise 1: We are saved by grace through faith, NOT by works (Ephesus 2:8-9). Premise 2: Baptism is a work. Conclusion: Therefore baptism can have no connection with salvation. Those who follow this argument rightly want to be true to the grace concept of salvation, but they have become *Zwinglianized*, i.e., deceived into thinking that embracing grace somehow requires giving up baptism as a salvation event.

How may we respond to this approach? Can we show that baptism as a salvation event is consistent with salvation by grace? YES! ABSOLUTELY! The question, then, is HOW can these two be reconciled? I will explain this in two steps, one following Luther and one following Paul!

I. LUTHER: BAPTISM **IS** A WORK, BUT IT IS NOT **OUR** WORK. IT IS **GOD'S** WORK.

This approach says that the controversial element in the Zwinglian revision is its second premise: "Baptism is a work." Luther's Zwinglian opponents challenged his adherence to the 1500-year consensus on baptism on these grounds. How can you say works are of no use for salvation, they asked him, and then say that baptism is for salvation? Is baptism itself not a work? What about faith? Here is Luther's stated answer to this challenge ("Large Catechism," IV.35): "To this you may answer: Yes, it is true that our works are of no use for salvation. Baptism, however is not our work but God's . . . . God's works are . . . necessary for salvation, and they do not exclude but rather demand faith."

I have often used Luther's excellent and Biblical reasoning on this issue. The fact is that every NT reference to baptism's meaning depicts it as accomplishing something that only God can perform (e.g., forgiveness, regeneration, baptism in the Spirit, resurrection from spiritual death). The only one really *working* in baptism is God; we come to it simply with "faith in the working of God" (Colossians 2:12). The one being baptized is passive, allowing something to be done TO himself or herself.

In the new Zwinglian view of baptism, God himself is doing NOTHING; the only significant work being done therein is by the one being baptized, for whom baptism is his or her response, commitment, expression, testimony, pledge, announcement, confirmation, or demonstration—all HUMAN works. In Scripture, though, NONE of these things is ever connected with baptism. The only things the baptized person is doing in baptism is believing (Colossians 2:12) and praying (Acts 22:16; 1 Peter 3:21)—both of which are indisputably consistent with grace. (The translation "pledge" in 1 Peter 3:21 is wrong.)

But is not baptism really a "work" in the simple sense of "something we do"? Would this not make it a work in the sense of

Ephesians 2:9, which excludes works from the way of salvation? The answer is NO, this is a faulty approach to the works issue. To see why this is so, we must make sure we are DEFINING the term "works" in the proper Pauline sense.

II. PAUL: BAPTISM IS OBEDIENCE TO THE GOSPEL, NOT A WORK OF LAW.

I have concluded that the main reason people think baptism for salvation and salvation by grace are contradictory is that they are using the wrong definition of "works" as used in Ephesians 2:8-9 and elsewhere in Paul's writings. It is uncritically assumed that a "work" is simply "something WE do," especially as opposed to something GOD does.

The fact is that "works" CAN be defined and used this way, *as Jesus himself uses "works" language in John 6:26-29.* But I have concluded on good evidence that this CANNOT be the sense of "works" as Paul uses the term, because this would put him in contradiction with Jesus in John 6:26-29. In this text Jesus uses "works" in the generic sense of "something we do," and he applies this terminology to FAITH ITSELF. Thus FAITH is a work in the sense of "something we do." But here is the kicker: Paul makes a clear distinction between faith and works (Romans 3:27-28; 4:4-5; Ephesians 2:8-9). This forces us to conclude that Paul must be using the term "works in a different sense. It cannot mean simply "something we do." For Paul, it must mean something more specific.

So what exactly DOES Paul mean when he uses the term "works"? Paul himself answer this question when he uses the more complete expression, "works of law" (as in Romans 3:20, 28; Galatians 2:16; 3:2, 5, 10). When you examine his "works" language closely in context, you will see that he always means "works of law," even when he says just "works" and does not add "of law."

So what are "works of law" in Paul's vocabulary? (Note that there are no articles in any of Paul's use of the phrase.) One thing he *cannot* mean is just the "Law of Moses," because in the Romans context he is including the Gentiles and Abraham in the discussion. The bottom line is this: for Paul, a "work" or "work of law" is ANY deed (external or internal, sinful or righteous) done in response to the law code that God as Creator has bound upon us as creatures. (Romans 3:28 through 4:8 shows that even sins belong in this definition.) Positively (as *good* works), works of law are just our acts of everyday obedience to God's teaching on how to live a holy life. They are acts of obedience to our law code. They are "living the Christian life."

Now here is a crucial point: in Paul's vocabulary, not all obedience to God is obedience to one's law code; not all "things we do" are the creature's response to God as Creator and his LAW commands. For Paul, some "things we do" are the sinner's response to God our Savior's GOSPEL commands, i.e., instructions to sinners on how to be saved. These are NOT "works of law," but are "obedience to the gospel." This latter is the expression Paul uses in Romans 10:16 (properly translated) and in 2 Thessalonians 1:8. When Paul is excluding "works" from the way of salvation, he is excluding "works of law," not "obedience to the gospel." The latter is fully consistent with grace.

What are the gospel commands directed toward sinners by God in his role as Savior, instructing sinners on how to receive salvation? (Whatever these are, they are NOT WORKS in Paul's sense of the term!) Here I would list the first four fingers of the venerable "five-finger exercise": faith, repentance, confession, and baptism. I would NOT include "living the Christian life," which counts instead as works of law.

Baptism thus is NOT a work, in Paul's sense and use of that term. He does NOT have baptism in mind when he writes Ephesians 2:8-9. Yes, baptism is "something we do" (just as faith is), but it is not something we do in response to a law command. "Be baptized" is a grace command, a gospel command. As an act of obedience to the gospel, baptism is just as consistent with grace as is faith.

Based on this Biblical analysis, it no longer makes any sense whatsoever to reject the Biblical view of baptism as a salvation event because of some alleged but unfounded contradiction with grace.

"Men and brethren, what shall we do?" We shall fully embrace both salvation by grace AND salvation in baptism, a la Luther and especially Paul. Also, we shall henceforth be honest and rational in our exegesis of NT teaching concerning baptism. Finally, we shall speak the truth in love regarding this subject of baptism. When we preach, teach, and write about baptism, we must be more concerned about what GOD thinks of our presentations than about what men think. "Let God be true though everyone were a liar" (Romans 3:4, ESV). Let God's WORD be true, though everyone were a liar. Let our PREACHING of God's Word be true, though everyone else were a liar.

10. FOR GOOD WORKS

I like to summarize salvation, using Ephesians 2:8-10 and Colossians 2:12, thus: we are saved BY GRACE, THROUGH FAITH, IN BAPTISM, FOR GOOD WORKS. Here we are examining the last phrase, "for good works" (Ephesians 2:10). Good works are simply our everyday obedience to God's law, i.e., being holy as God is holy, obeying our law code, living the Christian life, being good.

How do works (being good) fit into the salvation picture? Outside Christianity, and even for many within it, the general view is that we are saved BY works. (Paul wrote Romans 1-5 to combat this view.) On the other hand, many within Christendom have gone to the other extreme and have concluded that, since we are justified by faith, we don't need to do good works. Thus we are saved FROM works. (Paul wrote Romans 6 to combat this view.)

The Biblical view is different from both of these extremes. As Ephesians 2:10 says, we have been saved FOR good works. Understanding the difference between BY WORKS and FOR WORKS can make all the difference in the world for the Christian's life and hope. Being justified by faith does not do away with works, but it causes us to see them in a totally new way. It enables us to say the following three things about works.

ONE: The word of LIBERATION: "I CAN do good works – because of *grace*."

Until a person is saved, he or she cannot do good works. The second part of the "double curse" is that sin corrupts our hearts with spiritual sickness, even spiritual death (Jeremiah 17:9; Ephesians 2:1, 5). This applies not necessarily to external obedience, but to the states of our hearts: attitudes, motives, goals.

But grace changes this. As our "double cure," it not only resolves our legal problem of guilt and punishment, but also gives us a new nature that is in the process of being healed from sin-sickness. We have been given a new heart and a new spirit (Ezekiel 36:26); we are new creatures (2 Corinthians 5:17); "we are his workmanship, created in Christ Jesus for good works" (Ephesians 2:10). "His workmanship" is the work of regeneration and sanctification, accomplished mainly through the indwelling Holy Spirit.

It is because of the Spirit's work within us that we CAN obey! It is "by the Spirit" that we put sin to death in our bodies (Romans 8:13). God strengthens us with power through his Spirit working within our souls (Ephesians 3:16). We work out the sanctification part of our salvation through God the Spirit, who is at work within us, helping us both to want to do good and to actually do it (Philippians 2:12-13).

Why do so many Christians still have trouble with sin? Because they have not yet learned how to use the power of the Holy Spirit in their lives! This is a tragedy, like Clark Kent living his whole life without knowing he was Superman! Don't be like that: say, "I CAN DO GOOD WORKS, because God's grace is working in me!"

TWO: The word of OBLIGATION: "I OUGHT to do good works – because of *creation*."

Some think grace means that God's commands are no longer binding on us, and that we do not really HAVE TO obey his law! After all, we are not under law, but under grace! Doesn't Paul say that in Romans 6:14-15? Well, yes, but that is a *serious* misunderstanding of that text. Paul goes on to show in the verses that follow that even as Christians we are *slaves* to God and are therefore 100% obligated to obey every commandment of the law code that applies to us in this NT age.

Paul does not go into it here in Romans 6, but the ultimate basis for this obligation is the fact of creation. Everything—including us as persons—is God's possession because he is the Creator (Psalm 24:1-2). We owe God the debt of obedience just because he is the Creator. Grace does not change this.

So what does Romans 6:14-15 mean? It means we are not under the LAW SYSTEM as a WAY OF SALVATION. We are free from the requirement of perfect obedience as a way of getting to heaven. We are NOT, however, free from our law code as a WAY OF LIFE, as a binding code of conduct. We are still absolutely obligated to obey all of God's commands that regulate our everyday life. Freedom from law is NOT freedom from obedience. Is this legalism? NO! As Edward Fudge has said, legalism is law-

DEPENDING (depending on your obedience to save you). But we are talking about law-KEEPING, which simply means *holiness*. Jesus is not only our Savior; he is also our Lord.

So – "Do I HAVE to be good?" YES! "But do I have to be good as a way of getting into heaven?" NO! "So why should I care about being good?" First, because it's the right thing to do, totally apart from any consideration of heaven or hell. But there is much more than this; there is another word that we must say about good works:

THREE: The word of MOTIVATION: "I WILL do good works—because of *love*."

"OK, I *can* do good works. And OK, I *ought* to do good works. But *will* I?" Of course you will! How could you not? You are a Christian! You believe in Jesus! And FAITH WORKS (Galatians 5:6); that is its very nature. In fact, true faith not only works—it works HARD! It toils and labors.

Like English, Greek has two words for "work." One is ordinary work (*ergon;* verb *ergazomai*); the other is LABOR (*kopos; kopiaō*). Both words are used for the Christian life; see 1 Corinthians 15:58, which says we abound in the WORK of the Lord, since our LABOR is not in vain in him. Yes, we are willing to labor and toil for our Lord. As the old hymn "To the Work" says, "Toiling on, toiling on! Toiling on, toiling on! Let us hope, let us watch, and labor till the Master comes!"

But the question here is, what motivates the Christian to work so hard at fighting sin and being good? Those who think only in terms of law will say, we work in order to escape hell and go to heaven. OK, maybe we used to think that way, *but grace changes this motivation.* Remember: salvation by grace is a free gift (Romans 6:23; Ephesians 2:8-9), and we cannot work for a gift (Romans 4:4). Also, there is no hell for those who are in Jesus (Romans 8:1). So why DO we labor for our Lord? BECAUSE OF LOVE—grateful love. Jesus says if we love him, we will keep his commands (John 14:15). Paul affirms that faith works through love (Galatians 5:6); our Christian life is a "labor of love" (1 Thessalonians 1:3). See 1 John 4:18-19: the more we love, the less we work out of fear.

Grace does not change our obligation (why we OUGHT to obey), but it changes our motivation (why we DO obey). We obey not in order TO BE saved, but because we ARE saved. We are saved not BY works, but FOR works. Obedience is not a "got to" thing; it is a "get to" thing. Our good works are not sin offerings; they are thank offerings. "Jesus paid it ALL"—not just a down-payment. "All to him I owe"—as a debt of gratitude.

Many preachers think that if they do not tie works to salvation, Christians will neglect their moral responsibilities and church duties. But we need to remember that there is no stronger motive than love. A parent will risk all and enter a burning building to save a child. A bride will work hard to look her loveliest for her groom. When you love someone, you cannot do enough for that person; that is the very essence of *agapē.* The other side of that coin is that you would rather do anything in the world than to hurt the one you love. And we need to remember: sin is a wound in the heart of God. Love and sin do not mix. We need to teach our people how to love God.

We also need to remember that we are justified by the blood of Christ; this means that our sins and imperfections are covered by his blood (Romans 3:28; 4:6-8). We trust his atoning death to get us into heaven, not the record of our works. Let us stop focusing on and worrying about whether we are forgiven (which we are), and concentrate on our sanctification. Let us concentrate on pleasing God through good works, on striving to be holy as God is holy—because we LOVE GOD.

It boils down to this: good works are the result, not the cause, of our salvation. And: God does not save us because we are good, but we are good because God is saving us.

11. ABOVE AND BEYOND

Much of the world (including many Christians) assume that if we do something "wrong," we can do something "right" to make up for it. In many religions this concept is the key to whatever they consider to be "salvation." An example of this is the "balance-scale" concept of judgment. In this view every good work has a certain amount of merit attached to it; every sin has a certain amount of demerit. On the Judgment Day all good works are placed on one side of the scale and all bad works on the other. If "our good works outweigh our bad works" (as I heard a church deacon once pray), then we will be saved.

The idea that our good works can offset, make up for, or cancel out our sins is a very widespread idea. It is the essence of the Hindu concept of *karma*. It is prevalent in the Islamic idea of salvation. Here are some citations from Muslim writings: "Lo! Good deeds annul evil deeds." "Whoever has surrounded his ill deeds with his good deeds, his scale will be heavy. His good deeds will annul his evil deeds, and whoever has surrounded his good deeds with his evil deeds certainly his scale will be light, and he is a child of Hell. His ill deeds have annulled his good deeds." "If you have done an evil deed, then do along with it a good deed and this will erase it." (Quotes taken from a booklet by a converted Muslim, Iskander Jadeed, who cites sources. See *Sin and Atonement in Islam and Christianity*, Basel, 27, 31, 33.)

The Roman Catholic concept and practice of indulgences (as part of the sacrament once called penance, now reconciliation) includes this concept of "extra merit." Catholic doctrine says that the saints have more good works (more merit) than they need for themselves; all of this extra merit goes into a "treasury of merits" from which we may make withdrawals to cancel out the punishment for our venial (lesser) sins. We can make such withdrawals by doing our own good works, even though they have a lesser degree of merit. Together, our meritorious works (perhaps 5% of the needed merit) plus the saints' surplus merit (the other needed 95%) make up for our sin.

All such ideas assume that in our obedience to God, we can go "above and beyond the call of duty"; i.e., we can do something good that is somehow not needed for its own sake, and use it to pay our sin-debt to God. This is the concept of "extra merit."

The sad truth is this: in our life of obedience to God's laws, THERE IS NO SUCH THING AS EXTRA MERIT! There is no such thing as "going above and beyond the call of duty." This is an important lesson taught by Jesus in his parable of the "unprofitable servant" (Luke 17:7-10, NKJV): "And which of you, having a servant plowing or tending sheep, will say to him when he has come in from the field, 'Come at once and sit down to eat'? But will he not rather say to him, 'Prepare something for my supper, and gird yourself and serve me till I have eaten and drunk, and afterward you will eat and drink'? Does he thank that servant because he did the things that were commanded him? I think not. So likewise you, when you have done all those things which you are commanded, say, 'We are unprofitable servants. We have done what was our duty to do.'"

What is Jesus teaching here? He is showing us that as God's creatures we already owe him every good deed, every act of obedience that we can possibly do. This is our creature-debt; we owe the Creator the debt of perfect obedience to our law code. Perfection is our duty: "You therefore must be perfect, as your heavenly Father is perfect" (Matthew 5:48). "But as he who called you is holy, you also be holy in all your conduct" (1 Peter 1:15).

Here is what this means: even if we were living a perfect life, we would have no "profit," nothing above and beyond what is our duty to do. This further means that *we can never do something extra to make up for our sins!* Why not? Because every good thing we can possibly do is already owed to God as a requirement. When you do not do some good thing you are supposed to do (i.e., when you sin), this is like getting behind in the payment of your debt of obedience. Now in addition to owing God your ongoing debt of perfect obedience, you owe him the debt of penalty for disobedience. And once you get behind like this, YOU CAN NEVER CATCH UP! Why not? Because you will never have any extra good works (works not already owed to God) to apply to your sin-debt.

Here's an illustration. Let's say that when I met my future wife, I was so desperate to marry her that I willingly signed her shrewd prenuptial agreement. In this agreement I agreed to immediately transfer to her the ownership of EVERY THING and EVERY

PENNY I then possessed *and ever would possess* by no matter what means. Two years after we married, she discovered I had NOT been giving to her two dollars from my paycheck every week. I had been withholding it to sneak a Skyline chili once in a while. She rightfully demanded to know what I planned to do about the $104.00 I owed her. In despair I frantically promised I would soon repay her. In pity she looked at me and said, "What with?" (Fortunately this is only an illustration.)

The point of Jesus' parable is simply this: every act of obedience we can do is already owed to God as our creature-debt. We cannot use what we already owe via that debt, to pay off our sin-debt. Thus we have only two choices: (1) live a perfect life and "stay even," and thus avoid hell via our own works; or (2) sin just once and fall behind in our sin-debt forever. We all know where we stand.

How then can sinners be saved? ONLY BY GRACE – in the form of Jesus' perfect atonement for our sin. His propitiatory death is the only thing that can truly "make up for" our sin. His sacrifice for us is the only true "extra merit"; only Jesus has "gone above and beyond the call of duty." His "extra merits," earned via his death on the cross, are what go on the other side of the balance scale, canceling out our sins and giving us eternal life. "Not the labors of my hands can fulfill Thy law's demands. Could my tears forever flow; could my zeal no respite know! All for sin could not atone—THOU must save, and Thou alone."

Finally, I want to point out that the depiction of God in the "unprofitable servant" parable is very severe and stern and unyielding.

Is this what our God is truly like? Yes, but remember this: there are TWO SIDES to God's nature: his sternness (severity, holiness) and his kindness (goodness, love), as seen in Romans 11:22. This parable does represent the former. But see Luke 12:35-37, which shows how God treats sinners according to the GRACE side of his nature! Let us not forget the lesson of the parable in Luke 17, but let us rest our hope in God as he is shown in Luke 12. It is not WE who go above and beyond the call of duty, but GOD.

12. LIVING BY GRACE

Long ago I saw this comic strip: (Panel 1) – The boss bawls out his employee. (2) The employee goes home and hollers at his wife. (3) The wife yells at Junior. (4) Junior screams at the dog. (5) The dog growls at the goldfish. The scolding stops with the poor goldfish.

Here are two separate scenes of a little girl playing with her doll. Scene 1: The girl says to her doll, "You bad doll! You spilled your milk again! You're no good for anything! Can't you ever do anything right? Take that!" – as she slaps the doll on the side of its head. Scene 2: The girl says to her doll, "Oh, Dolly! You spilled your milk again! You must be more careful. There now, don't cry; Mommy still loves you. Here, let me give you a big kiss!" – as she picks up the doll and hugs it.

What's going on here? It's simple: people tend to treat one another the way others have treated them. Why do the little girls treat their dolls so differently? Because they are acting out toward their dolls the way THEIR mothers have treated them.

This idea helps to explain what it means to "grow in grace" (2 Peter 3:18). How does one grow in grace? This is not talking about how we RECEIVE a greater quantity of grace each day. Actually, it is a command. Growing in grace is something WE must DO. So what does it mean? I am suggesting that to grow in grace means that every day we as Christians must strive harder *to treat others the way God has treated us!*

We have seen how God has saved us and blessed us with his grace. He has given to us the wonderful gifts of forgiveness and the indwelling Spirit. We have gratefully received these blessings of his grace. Now what does God expect of us? Very simply, he expects us to LIVE BY THE SPIRIT OF GRACE toward other people—to be gracious to them—to develop a *lifestyle of grace.*

We know the "golden rule": do unto others as you would have them do unto you (Matthew 7:12). Now here is a similar rule, the "gracious rule": DO UNTO OTHERS AS GOD HAS DONE UNTO YOU! This gracious lifestyle is summed up in two words: GIVING and FORGIVING.

First, GRACE MEANS GIVING. The most basic meaning of the Greek word for grace, *charis,* is "a GIFT that brings joy." Giving is the very essence of grace. That God is gracious means that he is a giver (see James 1:17). It is his nature to give, and his greatest gift is grace itself (Ephesians 2:8-9; Romans 6:23). We have accepted this gift gladly. Now what? How must we respond? As Jesus said in Matthew 10:8, "Freely you have received, freely give."

What is the alternative to being a giver? That's easy: being a TAKER. A taker is someone who is always interested in what he can get out of others, i.e., how he can take advantage of them or exploit them. This includes husbands who treat their wives as slaves, and spoiled children. It includes those with a "What's in it for me?" attitude. It's the person who thinks like a dog we once owned. We decided her philosophy of life was "Everything that exists is here for ME—either to eat or chew on."

But if we are saved by grace, we cannot live like this! God wants us to be GIVERS. A skeptic once said, "I can't stand this Christianity business. All I ever hear from them is "Give, give, give!" The preacher to whom he was speaking answered, "That's about the best description of Christianity I have ever heard!" But it is not just about money, of course. It is about one's very heart or character. We must have a giving heart, a giving spirit. You can give a lot of money and still not be a giver.

We must work and pray for a giving heart. This will lead us to share our possessions with those in need (Luke 6:32-35). It will lead us to serve others with our talents and abilities (all of which are given to us by God—1 Corinthians 4:7). It will prepare us to be ready to give in many ways: to give others the credit for work done, to give others the benefit of the doubt, to give them another chance. It will help us to accept people without making them earn it.

An old hymn says, "I would be giving, and forget the gift." This is living by grace.

Second, GRACE MEANS FORGIVING. Are you a gracious person? Are you truly living by grace? The ultimate test of the gracious heart is this: how do you respond to people who have harmed you in some way? The response of grace is *forgiveness.*

Actually, nothing is more characteristic of grace than forgiveness. It is the greatest gift you can give. Forgiveness is the heart of the package of salvation God has given us: forgiveness of sins, remission of sins, justification. This is the way Jesus treated people, even his crucifiers: "Father, forgive them, for they do not know what they are doing" (Luke 23:34). His manner is summed up in Isaiah 42:3 and Matthew 12:20, "A bruised reed he will not break." Sinners are bruised reeds; they deserve to be broken off and discarded. WE are such bruised reeds, but Jesus is treating us with a forgiving heart, tenderly nursing us back to good spiritual health.

Now what? How must we respond? As the Apostle Paul specifically says, "Be kind to one another, tender-hearted, forgiving each other, just as God in Christ also has forgiven you" (Ephesians 4:32).

What is the alternative to being a forgiver? The answer is simple: being a BREAKER. I.e., when someone has hurt us, the common response is to desire to BREAK that person like a bruised reed: to strike back, to get even, to make him suffer or to cause him pain in some way. Let's be honest. When someone harms us or our family, what is our first impulse? Do we not want to break the offender in some way—to punish "that dirty rat"? Maybe not with physical harm, but via harsh words, insults, ridicule, the "silent treatment," or economic harm.

But here is where we must learn to LIVE BY GRACE. We must be forgivers, not breakers. "But they deserve my wrath!" Yes, perhaps so. But grace is the very opposite of treating people as they deserve.

Isn't that how God in his grace has treated us? This means that if someone has done us wrong or harmed us or ours, we will not continue to hold it against him or her, much less try to cause them overt pain. We will not want to hurt back or do things designed to "get even."

Here is a very important point: being personally gracious and forgiving toward offenders does NOT rule out LEGAL justice when this is warranted and when it is rightfully administered by our justice system. Remember the two sides to God's nature, i.e., holy wrath and loving grace. It is God's desire and prerogative to punish evildoers, and he has appointed civil government for that very purpose (Romans 13:1-4; 1 Peter 2:13-15). It is not wrong to want to see criminals punished. But God has appointed government to do that, and has forbidden us to take personal revenge (Romans 12:14-21). In our role as Christians we represent the church, and the church's job is to present the loving and forgiving side of God's nature to the world. The government lives by justice; we as individual Christians live by grace.

The bottom line is that we as Christians have no choice but to forgive. The so-called Christian who makes no attempt to forgive does not really understand what Christ and Christianity are all about, and can make no claim to God's grace (see Matthew 6:14-15). So let's take 2 Peter 3:18 seriously, and seek to GROW IN GRACE. We can do this by giving up the spirit of taking and breaking, and developing the spirit of giving and forgiving.

13. ORIGINAL SIN OR ORIGINAL GRACE?

What about babies—when they are conceived, while in the womb, at birth? Are they under law, or under grace? This question is actually raised and answered in Romans 5:12-19, where Adam's sin is contrasted with Christ's cross. The issue being settled here is simply this: which of these is stronger? Which prevails over the other?

At least since the time of Augustine (d. A.D. 430), the Christian world has tended to focus on what this text says about Adam more than what it says about Christ. Most see it as teaching the doctrine of ORIGINAL SIN. What does this phrase mean? It does not refer to an act, i.e., it does not refer to Adam and Eve's first sin. "Original sin" means a *condition*, the spiritual condition in which children are conceived and born. How is this condition understood, and what does it have to do with Adam? In fact, IS there such a thing as "original sin"?

First, how do we know that this text is even referring to little children? Basically because of vv. 12-14. Here Paul says Adam's sin causes all to die, "because ALL sinned" (aorist/past tense), EVEN "those who had not sinned in the likeness of the offense of Adam." The best understanding here is that the fact that sometimes even babies die is not because they sinned personally but because they sinned *representatively* in Adam in the Garden of Eden. (See my Commentary on Romans on these verses.)

Thus when Adam sinned, he was acting for all of us, as our representative. The question then is, how did this sin affect the entire human race? On a practical level, what is at stake here is the status of children when they are conceived and born. Do children come into existence in a state called "original sin"? Does the "death" brought upon all by Adam's sin include spiritual and eternal death?

I.   THE DOCTRINE OF ORIGINAL SIN

We will remember that sin causes two main problems (the "double curse"): the legal problem of guilt and condemnation to hell, and the spiritual condition of sinfulness or depravity. The earliest views of some form of original sin arose around A.D. 200, when some Christians began to believe that babies come into existence with a (partially) sinful, depraved nature. This view was later called "semi-Pelagianism," and some still hold to it. (This was Alexander Campbell's belief. See his *Christian System*, chapters 5-7.) It is a rather weak view of original sin.

It was Augustine who developed the full-fledged doctrine of original sin. He said babies come into existence not just partially depraved but TOTALLY depraved, meaning that they have no free will to accept any offer of salvation that might come to them later on. But that's not all. He also said that babies come into existence bearing the full guilt and condemnation of Adam's sin, and are thus bound for hell (unless they can be baptized). This complete doctrine of original sin was accepted by the major Reformers in the 16th century, and is still a central idea in Lutheranism and Calvinism.

This doctrine is tied in with Romans 5:12-19 because this text says all DIE because of Adam's sin, and this "death" seems to include not just physical death but also spiritual death (total depravity) and eternal death (condemnation to hell). Verse 15 says that the one man's sin brought death (of all kinds) to "the many." ("Many" in this passage is not being contrasted with "all," but with "one." It refers to the entire human race.) Verse 16 says the one sin brought judgment and condemnation, which must refer to eternity in hell. Verse 17 says "death reigned" through the one man. Verse 18 says the one sin brought "condemnation to all men." Verse 19 says that "through the one man's disobedience the many were made sinners."

The fact is that *Paul does say that all these things are brought on the whole human race because of Adam's sin!* Now what? What is the solution to this horrendous legacy of Adam? Defenders of original sin have suggested two ways that infants can be set free from this condition. The first and earliest solution was INFANT BAPTISM. In fact, this is why infant baptism was originally introduced, at the same time as ideas of original sin arose (c. A.D. 200). Augustine solidified this view; it was adopted by Roman Catholicism and later by Lutherans. (Most others baptize babies for other reasons, as originated by Huldreich Zwingli in the 1520s, even if they believe in original sin.)

The second answer to setting babies free from original sin is found mainly in Calvinism, namely, PREDESTINATION. I.e., all those whom God unconditionally predestines to be saved will be delivered from original sin whenever God chooses to do so (unconnected with baptism).

Neither of these solutions is acceptable. For one thing, both of them offer just a partial solution to the problem of original sin: only SOME infants are baptized, and only SOME are predestined to be saved (in these views). But this simply does not do justice to what Paul is saying here ABOUT JESUS CHRIST, and his ORIGINAL GRACE.

II. THE DOCTRINE OF ORIGINAL GRACE

The doctrine of original sin as described above misses the whole point of Romans 5:12-19. True, Paul does say that death, condemnation, and sin come upon ALL HUMAN BEINGS because of Adam's sin. But that is only part of what he says, and it is not even his main point. We need to focus on "the rest of the story" (as Paul Harvey used to say), which is this: *The clear teaching of Romans 5:12-19 is that the one act of redemption by the one man Jesus Christ not only wipes away ALL the effects of Adam's sin, but MUCH MORE* (vv. 15, 17). Thus Paul is NOT teaching the doctrine of original sin, but rather what we may call THE DOCTRINE OF ORIGINAL GRACE.

Paul's point is simply this: WHATEVER came upon (or WOULD have come upon) the entire race as infants as a result of Adam's sin, HAS BEEN REMOVED for the entire race as the result of the saving work of Jesus Christ and by the universal gift of saving grace. Thus when we think of the spiritual condition in which infants are conceived and born, we should think of them as being born NOT in original sin, but in the state of original grace.

The same verses in Romans 5 (vv. 15-19) that say all human beings got sin-consequences from Adam, say even more adamantly that all human beings got salvation-consequences from Christ. The latter completely cancel out the former. Verse 15 says all get death from Adam, but all get grace and the gift (of life) from Christ. (For babies who die, this is a guarantee of their future redemptive resurrection from the dead.) Verses 16 and 18 say all get condemnation from Adam, but all get justification from Christ. Verse 17 says all get death from Adam, but all get grace, righteousness, and life from Christ. Verse 19 says all are made sinners by Adam, but made righteous by Christ.

All of these blessings of original grace have been applied to all descendants of Adam, even from the beginning, even before the cross became an actual historical event. Were it not for God's "predetermined plan" (Acts 2:23) to send Jesus to the cross, thanks to Adam all babies WOULD have come into existence in original sin: sinful, guilty, and condemned. But instead, because of Christ, all babies come into existence in the state of original grace: pure, free, and innocent. This is true of all babies, not just some supposed "elect" and not just those "baptized." It is universal and automatic. (It does not result in universal salvation, since original grace erases only the results of ADAM'S sin, not the results of our own personal sins. Sins consciously committed can be removed only by grace consciously accepted when one hears the gospel.)

Here is how I think of babies and young children. When they come into existence, they enter into a world governed by law; but they themselves are wrapped in a cocoon of grace. As a result they are under the grace system, not the law system, until they reach the age of accountability. At that point the cocoon of grace dissolves, and the children are now responsible for their own personal sins and are under the law system. Now they need to hear and respond to the gospel to be saved from the consequences of their personal sins. If they accept the gospel they receive the gift of personal grace (the "much more" of vv. 15, 17).

To sum it up, the individual's spiritual odyssey begins with a theoretical original sin, which is canceled by Christ's original grace, which is (at the age of accountability) canceled by personal sin, which may then be covered by personal grace.

14. ONCE IN GRACE, ALWAYS IN GRACE?

"Once in grace, always in grace." "Once saved, always saved." "Eternal security."

These three phrases all refer to the same idea, namely, that once a person has truly become saved, he or she can never become unsaved. Once you are saved, you can never lose your salvation. The first person to teach this doctrine was Augustine (d. A.D. 430). He said, for example, "But now to the saints predestined to the kingdom of God by God's grace, ... perseverance itself is bestowed; ... so that by means of this gift they cannot help persevering" ("Treatise on Rebuke and Grace," *Works*, 15:103). This teaching continues in all Calvinism and in most Baptist groups.

I believe this is not only a false doctrine, but a SERIOUS false doctrine, for several reasons. One, it can give weak Christians a false sense of security and make them lax in their Christian life. Two, it keeps Christians from recognizing clear signs of apostasy. Three, it causes confusion concerning the genuine Biblical teaching concerning assurance. Four, it causes confusion about the role of free will in the Christian life.

Thus in this lesson I will summarize the Biblical teaching that it IS POSSIBLE for a Christian to lose his salvation. I will do so by examining the three stages in the life of the prodigal son as set forth by Jesus in parabolic form (Luke 15:11-32).

I. First Stage: The Prodigal Is ALIVE IN HIS FATHER'S HOUSE.

This parable is not about evangelism. The prodigal is not first depicted as a lost sinner, but as a full son and heir of the father. In the third stage of his life, when he returned home, he became "alive AGAIN" (v. 24), indicating that in this first stage he represents Christians who are spiritually alive in the church. Here, like the pre-prodigal, we have the free-will choice to STAY in the Father's house, or to LEAVE.

Referring to people who are already saved, the Bible makes it clear that *staying saved is conditional.* Here are a few texts that stress this conditionality by the use of the word "IF." First, see John 15:1-10, especially v. 6. Here Jesus is speaking specifically to his apostles (the eleven). In v. 4 he exhorts them to "abide in Me." This assumes they are already "in him," i.e., in a saving relationship with him. But this is a command, indicating their responsibility to STAY in him. Then in v. 6 he says, "IF [note the IF] anyone does not abide [remain, stay] in Me, he is thrown away as a branch and dries up; and they gather them, and cast them into the fire and they are burned." Literally they are "thrown outside." They WERE "inside," but because of their choice not to abide in him, they are "thrown outside "—and burned. This is not just a loss of rewards (a la 1 Corinthians 3:15), but the burning of the PERSON.

Another text showing conditionality is Romans 11:17-23. Here Paul says that Jews who refuse to believe in Jesus are like branches of an olive tree that are "broken off," while Gentiles who believe are like wild olive branches that have been grafted into the domesticated tree (the church) and are saved. The lost Jews have experienced God's severity, and the saved Gentiles have experienced his kindness. But then Paul warns these saved Gentiles that they will continue in their saved state "IF [note the 'if'] you continue in His kindness; otherwise you also will be cut off" (v. 22). This is a clear indication of the possibility that salvation can be lost.

Another "IF" text is 1 Corinthians 15:1-2, where Paul says the Corinthians will be saved "IF you hold fast the word which I preached to you, unless you believed in vain." Their present faith will become vain and useless for salvation IF they stop believing. See also Colossians 1:21-23, where Paul tells the Colossian Christians they will experience future salvation "IF [note the 'if'] indeed you continue in the faith firmly established and steadfast, and not moved away from the hope of the gospel."

We, like the prodigal, are presently ALIVE in the Father's house. Here we will stay IF we continue to be submissive in faith. God will guard us and keep us, but only as long as we continue to believe. See 1 Peter 1:5: we are "protected by the power of God through faith."

II. Second Stage: The Prodigal Is DEAD IN A FAR COUNTRY.

In salvation terms, when the prodigal was still in his Father's house (the church), he was truly saved. When he chose to leave of his own free will, he became truly lost (vv. 13-16). This is equivalent not to a pre-evangelized state but to the fallen-away state. His inheritance is gone (vv. 13-14). He is separated from his father, in a FAR COUNTRY. He is spiritually dead (vv. 24, 32). Is he still his father's son? Yes, but he is a DEAD son.

Just as the prodigal became dead in a far country, so the Bible speaks of the reality of a Christian's *falling from grace, falling away* from the saved state into a state of lostness. Romans 11:22 speaks of Jews who once were part of God's tree as "those who fell" when they refused to accept Jesus as their Messiah. In 1 Corinthians 9:27 Paul speaks of the possibility of even himself becoming "disqualified" in the race toward heaven. The Greek word he uses is *adokimos*, which means "reprobate" (see Romans 1:28; 2 Timothy 3:8). In Galatians 5:4 Paul speaks thus to the Judaizers: "You have been severed from Christ, you who are seeking to be justified by law; you have fallen from grace." They could not be SEVERED from Christ if they had not once been joined to him; they could not have FALLEN from grace if they had not once been standing in it. Second Peter chapter 2 compares certain false teachers with the "angels who fell" (v. 4), and says they have forsaken the right way and have gone astray (v. 15). See especially vv. 20-21.

The theme of the whole book of Hebrews is the possibility, danger, and foolishness of abandoning one's faith in Christ. If such abandonment is not possible, the whole book is a sham. See especially 6:4-8, where those truly saved (vv. 4-5) are warned against falling away and needing to be renewed AGAIN to repentance (v. 6).

There is no doubt about it: a Christian who is once ALIVE in the Father's house may become DEAD in the far country.

III. Third Stage: The Prodigal IS ALIVE AGAIN IN THE FATHER'S ARMS.

Again as a free-will choice, the prodigal is pictured as deciding to repent and return to his father's household (vv. 18ff.). He was dead in the far country, but now he is ALIVE AGAIN (vv. 24, 32). This answers the question of whether one who falls away can ever return. It shows that this is indeed possible, and this is confirmed by Romans 11:23, which says that fallen ones will be grafted back into the tree AGAIN if they do not continue in unbelief.

Hebrews 6:4-6 teaches the same thing when it is properly translated. Here a common wrong translation unfortunately leaves the opposite impression. This wrong translation says it is impossible to bring the fallen back to repentance, BECAUSE or SINCE they have re-crucified and shamed Christ. These last words, however, are present participles, and should be translated WHILE or AS LONG AS they are re-crucifying and shaming Christ. If they stop doing these things, they can indeed be renewed to repentance.

We conclude that "once in grace, always in grace" is a false doctrine. It is indeed possible for a saved person to lose his or her salvation. But how does this happen? The key is the fact that we are justified BY FAITH. We BECOME justified by faith, and we STAY justified by faith. Thus we stay forgiven and saved *as long as our faith in Jesus Christ and his atoning death remains alive.* If our faith dies (see James 2:17), we become unsaved.

We can keep our faith alive by avoiding the three situations which may cause our faith to die. One is SUDDEN (SPIRITUAL) SUICIDE, in which a person deliberately renounces his faith in Jesus because of new circumstances in his or her life. This seems to be the decision being contemplated by the recipients of the Book of Hebrews. Second, faith may die through SLOW STARVATION of the soul, in which our neglect of spiritual disciplines and church life deprives our faith of the nourishment needed to keep it alive (see Acts 2:42). Finally we must not allow our faith to be STRANGLED BY SIN, as depicted by Jesus in Matthew 13:7, 22. After conversion, to "deliberately keep on sinning" (Hebrews 10:26, NIV) will suck the life out of our faith (see Romans 8:13).

Made in the USA
Columbia, SC
22 February 2020

88197903R00074